THE
CONSTITUTIONAL
RIGHT
OF ASSOCIATION

THE
CONSTITUTIONAL
RIGHT
OF ASSOCIATION

David Fellman

THE UNIVERSITY OF CHICAGO PRESS

Library of Congress Catalog Card Number: 63-9728

THE UNIVERSITY OF CHICAGO PRESS, CHICAGO & LONDON
The University of Toronto Press, Toronto 5, Canada

FOR GARY

PREFACE

Text writers in American constitutional law have always assumed that the right of association is protected by the First
Amendment, and through the Due Process Clause, by the Fourteenth. But the real proportions of a constitutional right begin
to appear only as it is being challenged or violated. So long as
it was taken for granted, and went unnoticed, there seemed
little point in talking about it. But now that the right of association has been challenged, notably by the federal statutes dealing
with subversive organizations and the Southern assault upon the
National Association for the Advancement of Colored People,
the judges have had to think through the metes and bounds of
the right of association.

In the crucible of experience the term is acquiring definition
and proportions. This seems to be a good time, therefore, to try
one's hand at a systematic exploration of the concept. The purpose of this book is to spell out, in a preliminary way, the meaning of the constitutional guaranty of the right of association.
Since there are few established patterns of analysis in connection with the law writing on this subject, the various facets of
the problem will have to be worked out by writers as they go
along.

About half of this little book was first published, in somewhat abbreviated form, in *The Supreme Court Review* for
1961, published by the University of Chicago Press. I am in-
debted to its editor, Professor Philip B. Kurland, for permission
to reprint the materials used there. In addition, the second part
of chapter v was originally published *sub nom.* "Association

with 'Bad' People," in the *Journal of Politics* for November, 1960, Volume 22, pages 620–28. I am grateful to the editor of that estimable journal for his kind permission to include this essay in my book.

The right of association poses many problems which are scarcely touched upon in this book. Human associations involve sociological, political, economic, and psychological considerations of the greatest complexity. I say this to underscore the fact that all I have attempted here is to examine the legal aspects of the subject, and largely only those legal matters which fall within the ambit of public law. This is an essay in American constitutional law, but not much more. I suspect that if various specialists nibble away at the problem long enough, and seriously enough, we shall some day accumulate the materials and concepts necessary for a truly comprehensive study of the right of association.

I should like to take this opportunity to thank Professor Kurland, of the faculty of the Law School of the University of Chicago, for his invaluable assistance in preparing a good part of the manuscript for publication. He wields a very sharp editorial pencil.

CONTENTS

CHAPTER I

A HISTORICAL NOTE

"In no country in the world," Tocqueville wrote in his celebrated book on American democracy, "has the principle of
association been more successfully used or applied to a greater
multitude of objects than in America."[1] What was true over a
century ago is even more true today. Many writers have drawn
attention to the extraordinary multiplicity of interest groups in
the United States, to the American insistence upon voluntary
group action by private citizens, and indeed, to the American
passion for being a joiner.[2] It is not surprising, therefore, that
however ill-defined they may be, the rights of association have

[1] Alexis de Tocqueville, *Democracy in America*, ed. Phillips Bradley
(New York: Knopf, 1948), I, 191.

[2] See W. Willard Wirtz, "Government by Private Groups," *Louisiana
Law Review*, XIII (March, 1953), 440–75; Arthur M. Schlesinger, "Biog-
raphy of a Nation of Joiners," *American Historical Review*, L (October,
1944), 1–25, reprinted in *Paths to the Present* (New York: Macmillan,
1949), chap. ii; Walter Gellhorn, *American Rights* (New York: Macmillan, 1960), chap. ix; Charles Merz, *The Great American Band-Wagon*
(New York: John Day, 1928); Symposium on "Group Interests and the
Law," *Rutgers Law Review*, XIII (Spring, 1959), 429–602; Editors of
Fortune, U.S.A.; The Permanent Revolution (New York: Prentice-Hall,
1951): "There are at least 200,000 organizations, associations, clubs, societies, lodges, and fraternities in the United States, along with innumer-
able social groups and *ad hoc* committees formed for specific causes. . . .
This prodigious array of volunteer citizens . . . is unique in the world"
(*ibid.*, pp. 131–32).

a definite place in American constitutional law.[3] In fact, among American associations will be found many which exercise the right of association for the specific purpose of protecting the right to have rights.[4]

Tocqueville emphasized the liberty of political association, which he said had become "a necessary guarantee against the tyranny of the majority," especially needed in democratic countries to prevent the abuse of political power.[5] He noted that the right of political association involves, first, a number of individuals who give public assent to certain doctrines; second, the power of meeting; and third, the uniting into electoral bodies to choose representatives in a central assembly. In his view, therefore, association became in effect a government within the government. He concluded:

The most natural privilege of man, next to the right of acting for himself, is that of combining his exertions with those of his fellow creatures and of acting in common with them. The right of association therefore appears to me almost as inalienable in its nature as the right of personal liberty. No legislator can attack it without impairing the foundations of society.[6]

Tocqueville also drew attention to the fact that political associations may be dangerous, as in Europe, where they are weapons of conflict and direct action. In fact, he might have pointed out that every type of association has at some time been regarded as subversive, such as the dissenting churches of the sixteenth and seventeenth centuries, labor unions in the eighteenth and nineteenth centuries, and various fraternal groups

[3] See Glenn Abernathy, *The Right of Assembly and Association* (Columbia: University of South Carolina Press, 1961); Robert A. Horn, *Groups and the Constitution* (Stanford: Stanford University Press, 1956); Glenn Abernathy, "The Right of Association," *South Carolina Law Review*, VI (September, 1953), 32–77; Charles E. Wyzanski, Jr., "The Open Window and the Open Door," *California Law Review*, XXXV (September, 1947), 336–51.

[4] See Joseph B. Robison, "Organizations Promoting Civil Rights and Liberties," *Annals of the American Academy*, CCLXXV (May, 1951), 18–26; Clement E. Vose, "Litigation as a Form of Pressure Group Activity," *Annals of the American Academy*, CCCXIX (September, 1958), 20–31; Note, "Class Actions: A Study of Group-Interest Litigation," *Race Relations Law Reporter*, I (October, 1956), 991–1010.

[5] Tocqueville, *op. cit.*, I, pp. 194–95.   [6] *Ibid.*, p. 196.

throughout modern history.[7] But Tocqueville thought that in America private political associations were salutary. He found that their intentions were peaceful, and that they employed strictly legal methods. He also noted that universal suffrage made a difference since associations knew that they did not represent the majority of the nation.

The Supreme Court once took the position that the right of the people to assemble for lawful purposes existed long before the adoption of the Constitution. Speaking for the Court in the famous Reconstruction case, *United States* v. *Cruikshank*,[8] Mr. Chief Justice Waite wrote: "The very idea of a government, republican in form, implies a right on the part of its citizens to meet peaceably for consultation in respect to public affairs and to petition for a redress of grievances." Accordingly, the Court ruled that the right of assembly did not owe its origin to the Constitution, and that the purpose of the constitutional provision on the subject was simply to give additional security to a pre-existing right against its invasion by the national government.

The right of association is not, in so many words, mentioned in the national or state constitutions. The First Amendment of the national Constitution states that Congress shall make no law abridging "the right of the people peaceably to assemble, and to petition the Government for a redress of grievances." The broader rights of association have developed, in part, out of the right of assembly, and in part out of broader due process concepts. Historically, the right of assembly was closely connected with the right of petition. Mentioned as early as Magna

[7] See Horn, *op. cit.*, pp. 122–24. The Star Chamber regarded as illegal any unlicensed combination of men whose purposes were considered contrary to public policy by the judges, even though the acts involved were neither tortious nor indictable crimes. W. S. Holdsworth, *A History of English Law* (Boston: Little, Brown & Co., 1926), VIII, 382–83. Thomas Hobbes wrote in *Leviathan* (Pt. II, chap. xxii; Everyman's ed., p. 124): "Leagues of the Subjects of one and the same Common-wealth, where every one may obtain his right by means of the Sovereign Power, are unnecessary to the maintaining of Peace and Justice, and (in case the designe of them be evill, or Unknown to the Common-wealth) unlawful. For all uniting of strength by private men, is, if for evill intent, unjust; if for intent unknown, dangerous to the Publique, and unjustly concealed."

[8] 92 U.S. 542, 552 (1876).

Carta (1215),[9] the right of petition was important in English constitutional history because it was through the device of the petition that the barons and commons in Parliament first asserted the right to assume the initiative in legislation.[10] The king summoned Parliament to supply funds for the support of government, and Parliament, especially the House of Commons, quickly got into the habit of petitioning the Crown for a redress of grievances as the condition for voting the money. In addition, as a court of justice Parliament received petitions from many different sources, both individuals and communities, for all sorts of remedies not within the province of the regular courts.

Gradually the petition evolved into the legislative bill, so that by 1414 the Commons were able to assert to the King "that there should no statute or law be made unless they gave thereto their assent," since they were "as well assenters as petitioners."[11] The King agreed not to alter the petitions of the Commons. In 1669 the Commons resolved: "That it is an inherent right of every commoner of England to prepare and present Petitions to the house of commons in case of grievances, and the house of commons to receive the same . . . ;" further, "That it is the undoubted right and privilege of the commons to judge and determine concerning the nature and matter of such Petitions, how far they are fit or unfit to be received . . . ;" and finally, "That no court whatsoever hath power to judge or censure any Petition presented to the house of commons, and received by

[9] Chap. 61: "That if, we, our justiciary, our bailiffs, or any of our officers, shall in any circumstances have failed in the performance of them toward any person, or shall have broken through any of these articles of peace and security, and the offence be notified to four barons chosen out of the five-and-twenty before mentioned, the said four barons shall repair to us, or our justiciary, if we are out of the realm, and laying open the grievance, shall petition to have it redressed without delay." See W. S. McKechnie, *Magna Carta* (2d ed., Glasgow: Jas. Maclehose & Sons, 1914), pp. 465–77.

[10] See A. F. Pollard, *The Evolution of Parliament* (London: Longmans, Green, 1920), pp. 329–31.

[11] For the text see George B. Adams and H. Morse Stephens, *Select Documents of English Constitutional History* (New York: Macmillan, 1916), pp. 181–82. Down to Tudor times the words petition and bill were regarded as synonymous in common speech. C. H. McIlwain, *The High Court of Parliament* (New Haven: Yale University Press, 1910), p. 211.

them, unless transmitted from thence, or the matter complained of by them. . . ."[12] The right of petition received its classic modern formulation in the Bill of Rights of 1689, which declared "That it is the right of the subjects to petition the king and all commitments and prosecutions for such petitioning are illegal."[13]

While historically the right of peaceable assembly was regarded as a by-product of the right of petition, and was so once described by the Supreme Court,[14] it is now regarded, as Chief Justice Hughes said in 1937, as

. . . cognate to those of free speech and free press and is equally fundamental. . . . [T]he right is one that cannot be denied without violating those fundamental principles of liberty and justice which lie at the base of all civil and political institutions. . . . The greater the importance of safeguarding the community from incitements to the overthrow of our institutions by force and violence, the more imperative is the need to preserve inviolate the constitutional rights of free speech, free press and free assembly in order to maintain the opportunity for free political discussion, to the end that government may be responsive to the will of the people and that changes, if desired, may be obtained by peaceful means. Therein lies the security of the Republic, the very foundation of constitutional government.[15]

That the rights of peaceful assembly and petition had deep roots in the American experience was reflected in the frequency with which they were asserted in the formative period of American history. Thus, the Stamp Act Congress of 1765 asserted "That it is the right of the British subjects in these colonies to petition the King or either House of Parliament." (Resolution XIII). The First Continental Congress, on October 14, 1774, adopted a "Declaration and Resolves" which, among other things, asserted that the Americans "have a right peaceably to assemble, consider their grievances, and petition the King; and that all prosecutions, prohibitory proclamations,

---

[12] 4 Cobbett's *Parl. Deb.*, 432–33 (1669). See K. Smellie, "Right of Petition," *Encyclopaedia of the Social Sciences*, XII (1934), 99.

[13] Adams and Stephens, *op. cit.*, p. 464.

[14] See *United States* v. *Cruikshank*, 92 U.S. 542, 552 (1876).

[15] *De Jonge* v. *Oregon*, 299 U.S. 353, 364–65 (1937).

and commitments for the same, are illegal." (Eighth Resolution). The Declaration of Independence recited that "In every stage of these Oppressions We have Petitioned for Redress in the most humble terms. Our repeated Petitions have been answered only by repeated injury." Four of the revolutionary state constitutions, those of North Carolina, Massachusetts, New Hampshire, and Pennsylvania, spelled out a guaranty of the rights to assemble and petition. Thus, the North Carolina Constitution of 1776 declared: "That the people have a right to assemble together, to consult for their common good, to instruct their Representatives, and to apply to the Legislature, for redress of grievances."[16]

The federal constitutional Convention of 1787 did not include a bill of rights in the finished document, although a few delegates thought that this was a mistake. When the report of the Convention was before the Articles of Confederation Congress for consideration, prior to the submission of the proposed Constitution to the states for ratification, Richard Henry Lee tried, without success, to attach a bill of rights. Among such basic rights as freedom of the conscience and press, trial by jury, and free elections, he included the right of assembly.[17] When the states ratified the Constitution, eight of them formulated amendments which they wanted to add to it, and four of these included a guaranty of the rights of assembly and petition.[18] After the Constitution was ratified and put into effect,

[16] N.C. Const. (1776), Decl. of Rights, Art. 18. Cf. Penna. Const. (1790), Decl. of Rights, Art. IX, § 20: "That the citizens have a right, in a peaceable manner, to assemble together for their common good, and to apply to those invested with the powers of government for redress of grievances, or other proper purposes, by petition, address, or remonstrance." On this subject, Mass. Const. (1780), Decl. of Rights, Art. 19, and N.H. Const. (1784), Bill of Rights, Art. 32, were almost identical: "The people have a right in an orderly and peaceable manner, to assemble to consult upon the common good. . . ."

[17] James Curtis Ballagh (ed.), Letters of Richard Henry Lee (New York: Macmillan, 1911–14), II, 439, 442–44.

[18] Virginia Convention, June 27, 1788: "Fifteenth, That the people have a right peaceably to assemble together to consult for the common good, or to instruct their Representatives; and that every freeman has a right to petition or apply to the legislature for redress of grievances." New York Convention, July 26, 1788: "That the People have a right peaceably

James Madison initiated the movement for adding a bill of rights to the Constitution by proposing a series of amendments in the House of Representatives on June 8, 1789. He proposed, among other things, to include the following provision: "The people shall not be restrained from peaceably assembling and consulting for their common good; nor from applying to the Legislature by petitions, or remonstrances, for redress of their grievances."[19] When the amendments were reported by the Select Committee on July 28, 1789, this language had taken the following form: "The freedom of speech, and of the press, and the right of the people peaceably to assemble and consult for their common good, and to apply to the government for redress of grievances, shall not be infringed."[20] It was in this form that the amendment passed the House of Representatives on August 24, 1789.

But this did not occur until the subject was debated on Saturday, August 15, and Monday, August 17.[21] The Saturday debate centered on a proposal made by Representative Theodore Sedgwick of Massachusetts to delete the words "assembly and" from the clause, on the ground that the inclusion of the right of assembly with the rights of speech and press was improper and unwise because the former is too trifling and too obvious. "If people freely converse together, they meet to assemble for that purpose; it is a self-evident, inalienable right which the

---

to assemble together to consult for their common good, or to instruct their Representatives; and that every person has a right to Petition or apply to the Legislature for redress of Grievances." North Carolina Convention, August 1, 1788: "15th. That the people have a right peaceably to assemble together to consult for the common good, or to instruct their representatives; and that every freeman has a right to petition or apply to the Legislature for redress of grievances." Maryland Convention (Minority Report), April 29, 1788: "14. That every man hath a right to petition the legislature for the redress of grievances, in a peaceable and orderly manner." The texts of the state proposals for amending the Constitution are conveniently gathered together by Edward Dumbauld, *The Bill of Rights* (Norman: University of Oklahoma Press, 1957), pp. 173-205.

[19] See Dumbauld, *op. cit.*, p. 207.

[20] See *ibid.*, p. 210.

[21] For the best account we have of what was said on this occasion see *Annals of Congress*, I (1789), 731-47.

7

people possess; it is certainly a thing that never would be called in question." He said that it was like listing the right to put on your hat, and insisted that "it is derogatory to the dignity of the House to descend to such minutiae."[22] But several members of the House opposed Congressmen Sedgwick's motion. Egbert Benson of New York thought it was wise to secure an inherent right of the people against infringement by government. Thomas Tudor Tucker of South Carolina expressed the hope that the words would not be struck out, and both Elbridge Gerry of Massachusetts and Thomas Hartley of Pennsylvania called attention to the fact that the right of assembly was already in several state constitutions. John Vining of Delaware stated that incorporation of these words would gratify the states. Congressman John Page of Virginia called attention to the fact that the right of people to assemble together on lawful occasions had been violated in the past and ought to be safeguarded. "If the people could be deprived of the power of assembling under any pretext whatsoever," he declared, "they might be deprived of every other privilege contained in the clause." The record of Congress shows that following this brief debate, the motion to strike the words "assembly and" failed "by a considerable majority."[23] Thus the arguments for including a clause securing the right of assembly came to this: it is an important, indeed essential, and inherent right belonging to the people; there had been governmental invasions of it in the past; it was then included in several state constitutions; and if it is harmless, at least its inclusion will gratify the states.

The rest of the debate on the right-of-assembly clause centered on a motion by Congressman Tucker to add the words "to instruct their representatives." The right of the people to instruct their legislative representatives had deep roots in colonial practice,[24] and the Tucker motion touched off an interesting debate on the theory of the function of the representative. Mr. Hartley argued vigorously against the motion on the ground that representatives should be presumed to know the

---

[22] *Ibid.*, p. 731.   [23] *Ibid.*, p. 733.

[24] Hubert Phillips, *The Development of a Residential Qualification for Representatives in Colonial Legislatures* (Cincinnati: Abingdon Press, 1921).

interests and circumstances of their constituents and to have their confidence. He also doubted whether the people of a locality would be sufficiently well-informed to understand the needs of the nation as a whole, and he feared that if the representative listened to all the voices in his constituency, he would find it impossible to accommodate so many different desires.[25] In reply, Congressman Page argued that without the power to instruct their representatives, the people would be unable to consult for the common good. He made the point, then widely held, that instruction and representation were inseparable. Congressman Gerry maintained that even if instructions were specifically spelled out in the Constitution, the representative would still be at liberty to act as he pleased, but he could see no harm in putting in the right of instruction, if only thus to encourage people, and particularly the diffident, "to come forward with their instructions, which will form a fund of useful information for the Legislature."[26] But the contrary view prevailed. James Madison argued that the added words could do no "real good" because the people already had the right to communicate their sentiments and wishes to their representatives. Congressman William L. Smith of South Carolina thought that Tucker's proposal would be a partial inconvenience to the more distant states, and Michael Jenifer Stone of Maryland went so far as to assert that it would change government entirely from a representative system to a "democracy of singular properties."[27] Perhaps the most telling argument, which several members made, was that if the representatives adopt laws which are not satisfactory to the people, the people already have it within their power to withdraw their support and vote for others.

Today, a clause guaranteeing the rights of assembly and petition is found not only in the national Constitution, but also in those of all but four[28] state constitutions. That such a guaranty is not out of style is reflected in the fact that it is to be found in the shiny new constitutions of the recently-admitted states

[25] *Annals of Congress,* I, 733–35.

[26] *Ibid.,* p. 737.   [27] *Ibid.,* p. 739.

[28] Maryland, Minnesota, New Mexico, and Virginia do not make constitutional provision for this subject.

of Alaska and Hawaii.[29] A clause which includes most of the stock phrases is that in the Constitution of Texas, which reads as follows: "The citizens shall have the right, in a peaceable manner, to assemble together for their common good; and apply to those invested with the powers of government for redress of grievances or other purposes, by petition, address or remonstrance."[30] Almost all state constitutional clauses on this subject speak of "peaceful" or "orderly" assembly, or the right to assemble "peaceably." The vast majority also speak of the purpose of assembly, whether "to consult for the common good," or "to apply to the state government," or "to instruct their representatives." Finally, a large majority describe the method to be used, generally by "petition," though such phrases as "remonstrance" and "address" are also used.

In the course of deciding an appeal in an antitrust action, in 1961, a unanimous Supreme Court had occasion to record quite fully its appreciation of the right of petition.[31] The case was a chapter in the struggle between the truckers and the railroads for freight business. Forty-one Pennsylvania truck operators and their trade association filed an action against 24 eastern railroads, and their public relations firm, charging violation of Sections 1 and 2 of the Sherman Act. Conspiracy was alleged, and the allegation was that the railroads had engaged the public relations firm to conduct a publicity campaign against the truckers in order to secure the adoption and enforcement of laws which would hurt the trucking business. The charge was that the railroads were trying to create an unfavorable atmosphere for the truckers, and to impair relationships existing between the general public and their customers on the one hand, and the truckers on the other. It was alleged that the publicity campaign conducted by the railroads was "vicious, corrupt, and fraudulent." It was also alleged that the railroads utilized

[29] Alaska Const., Art. I, § 6: "The right of the people peaceably to assemble, and to petition the government shall never be abridged." Hawaii Const., Art. I, § 3: "No law shall be enacted . . . abridging . . . the right of the people peaceably to assemble and to petition the government for a redress of grievances."

[30] Texas Const., Art. I, § 27.

[31] *Eastern Railroad Presidents Conference* v. *Noerr Motor Freight, Inc.*, 365 U.S. 127 (1961).

the so-called third-party technique, which means that publicity matter circulated in the campaign was made to appear as the spontaneously expressed views of independent persons and civic groups when, in fact, the material was largely produced by the public relations firm and paid for by the railroads. There were also specific charges of particular instances in which the railroads had attempted to influence legislation by means of their publicity campaign. For example, one charge was that the railroads succeeded in persuading the Governor of Pennsylvania to veto a Fair Truck Bill which would have permitted the truckers to carry heavier loads. The railroads filed a counterclaim in this case, alleging that the truckers had used the same methods for the same ends. The federal district court and the court of appeals both ruled that the railroads had violated the Sherman Act, but that the truckers had not.

The Supreme Court reversed, holding that no violation of the Sherman Act "can be predicated upon mere attempts to influence the passage or enforcement of laws." There can be no violation of the statute where the restraint upon competition is the result of valid governmental action, as opposed to private action. But the Court thought it was "equally clear that the Sherman Act does not prohibit two or more persons from associating together in an attempt to persuade the legislature or the executive to take particular action with respect to a law that would produce a restraint or a monopoly." To hold otherwise would substantially impair the power of government to take action with regard to trade. In a representative democracy, said Mr. Justice Black, government must act on behalf of the people, "and, to a very large extent, the whole concept of representation depends upon the ability of the people to make their wishes known to their representatives." Any other construction would raise grave constitutional questions, since "the right of petition is one of the freedoms protected by the Bill of Rights, and we cannot, of course, lightly impute to Congress an intent to invade these freedoms." Thus it was noted that lawful conduct does not become a violation of the Sherman Act because the purpose of the railroads was to influence the passage and enforcement of laws designed to hurt or even destroy the truckers as competitors. Said Mr. Justice Black: "The right of the people to inform their representatives in government of their desires with respect to the passage or enforcement of laws cannot properly be made to depend upon their intent in doing so. It is neither unusual nor illegal for people to seek action on laws in the hope that they may bring about an advantage to themselves and a disadvantage to their competitors." Furthermore, "a construction of the Sherman Act that would disqualify people from taking a public position on matters in which they are financially interested would thus deprive the government of a valuable source of information and, at the same time, deprive the people of their right to petition in the very instances in which that right may be of the most importance to them."

As for the use of third-party techniques, while agreeing that it was unethical, the Court did not think that it was a violation of the Sherman Act. Insofar as the statute is concerned with ethics at all, it deals with trade restraints and not with political activity. A publicity campaign designed to influence government action clearly falls into the category of political activity. It was also pointed out that Congress has always used extreme caution in legislating with regard to political activities. Accordingly the Court felt that the use of the third-party technique was "legally irrelevant."

All in all, this was a rather resounding affirmation of a legal right which has almost never been involved in litigation, the right of petition. It will also be noted that the right of petition was closely allied in this case with the right of people to associate together in order to make their activities effective.

CHAPTER II

UNLAWFUL ASSEMBLY
AND PUBLIC MEETINGS

UNLAWFUL ASSEMBLY

Like all other rights, the right of assembly does not and cannot exist without limitation. "Although the rights of free speech and assembly are fundamental," Justice Brandeis once wrote, "they are not in their nature absolute. Their exercise is subject to restriction, if the particular restriction proposed is required in order to protect the State from destruction or from serious injury, political, economic or moral."[1] Thus, the doctrine of freedom of association does not apply to an alliance for crime, and one who knowingly joins an association with criminal purposes is a criminal.[2] The law of unlawful conspiracy limits the freedom of association.[3] The right to assemble and petition may be limited by the requirements of public order and public peace. Thus, in 1894 the leaders of General Jacob Coxey's famous march of the unemployed on Washington were

---

[1] *Whitney* v. *California*, 274 U.S. 357, 373 (1927) (concurring opinion). See Richard C. Barrett, "Limitations on the Right of Assembly," *California Law Review*, XXIII (January, 1935), 180–93; Zechariah Chafee, Jr., "Right of Assembly," *Encyclopaedia of the Social Sciences*, II (1930–35), 275–76.

[2] See *United States* v. *Socony-Vacuum Oil Co.*, 310 U.S. 150 (1940); *United States* v. *Crimmins*, 123 F. 2d 271 (2d Cir. 1941); *Momand* v. *Universal Film Exchange*, 6 F.R.D. 409 (D. Mass. 1947).

[3] See Rollin M. Perkins, *Criminal Law* (Brooklyn: The Foundation Press, 1957), pp. 546–48; William L. Clark and William L. Marshall, *A Treatise on the Law of Crimes*, ed. M. F. Wingersky (6th ed.; Chicago: Callaghan & Co., 1958), pp. 489–522.

arrested for walking unlawfully on the grass of the capitol. Similarly the camps of the veterans who marched on Washington in 1932 demanding bonus legislation were destroyed by the army as public nuisances. Breach of the peace, riot, and use of unlawful force are all considerations which set limits to the right of assembly.

Above all, the right of assembly is qualified by the concept of unlawful assembly. In American jurisdictions unlawful assembly is generally defined as a gathering of three or more people which has the common intent to attain a purpose, whether lawful or unlawful, that will interfere with the rights of others by committing acts in such fashion as to give firm and courageous people in the neighborhood reasonable ground to apprehend a breach of the peace.[4] Generally speaking, an unlawful assembly which breaches the peace but fails of its unlawful design is a rout; it is a riot when the illegal purpose is actually executed.[5] It has been stressed that to constitute a riot there must be a gathering which disturbs the peace, of three or more persons "unlawfully assembled together and acting in a violent and tumultuous manner."[6]

It has been emphasized by American courts that to sustain the charge of unlawful assembly, it must be alleged and proved, first that the defendants "assembled together," and that they intended to do an unlawful act or a lawful act in a violent, boisterous, or tumultuous manner.[7] Intimidation and threats are unlawful acts,[8] as well as the urging of boycotts and the making of personal attacks.[9] Furthermore, there may be an unlaw-

[4] See Clark and Marshall, *op. cit.*, pp. 523–25; *American Jurisprudence,* XLVI, 126; *People* v. *Kerrick,* 86 Cal. App. 542, 261 P. 756 (1927).

[5] A large and aggravated riot is often called a mob. At the common law the crime of unlawful assembly was an included offense of the crime of riot. *State* v. *Woolman,* 84 Utah 23, 33 P. 2d 640, 93 A.L.R. 723 (1934).

[6] *State* v. *Lustig,* 13 N.J. Super. 149, 80 A. 2d 309 (1951); *State* v. *Cole,* 2 McCord 73 (S.C. Law, 1822); *Slater* v. *Wood,* 9 Bosw. 15 (N.Y. Sup. Ct. 1861).

[7] *State* v. *Woolman,* 84 Utah 23, 33 P. 2d 640, 93 A.L.R. 723 (1934); *Aron* v. *Wausau,* 98 Wis. 592, 74 N.W. 354, 40 L.R.A. 733 (1898).

[8] *State* v. *Gennis,* 41 N.M. 453, 70 P. 2d 902 (1937).

[9] *American League of the Friends of the New Germany of Hudson County* v. *Eastmead,* 174 A. 156 (N.J. Chancery, 1934).

ful assembly even though there was no specific intent in the minds of those who assembled to act unlawfully, for unlawfulness may depend solely upon the numbers involved and their demeanor, so that the illegal purpose may have developed after the assembling.[10]

In 1891, the New York Court of Appeals went about as far as American courts are ever likely to go, in *People* v. *Most*.[11] Most had made a speech at a meeting held to protest the execution of ten Chicago anarchists who had been involved in the celebrated Haymarket affair. In his speech he glorified the deeds of the anarchists, denounced and threatened with death the officers connected with the case, and called upon his listeners to arm and resist the authorities. The people in the assembly indicated their agreement by applause. The Court of Appeals sustained a conviction for unlawful assembly under a statute which defined the offense as consisting of any attempt or threat on the part of three or more persons to do any act "tending towards a breach of the peace or an injury to person or property, or any unlawful act." The court held that it was not decisive that only one man did the talking, since, if two or more other people indicated agreement in some fashion, the requisite of the crime is met. Furthermore, the court did not believe it conclusive that the acts threatened were to happen in the future. The purpose of the statute is to protect the public peace, and such incendiary speeches as that of Most are not less dangerous merely because it is said that the time is not ripe for action. No one, said the court, can foresee the consequences of using such incendiary language before a crowd of ignorant and misguided men.

On the other hand, it is clear that a meeting cannot be prohibited merely because changes which are shocking or highly unpopular may be advocated.[12] The right of free public assembly, for the "free and open discussion of public questions" at stake in an election, may not be denied where there is no dis-

[10] *People* v. *Kerrick*, 86 Cal. App. 542, 261 P. 756 (1927).

[11] 128 N.Y. 108, 27 N.E. 970 (1891), Andrews, J.

[12] *American League of the Friends of the New Germany of Hudson County* v. *Eastmead*, 174 A. 156 (N.J. Chancery, 1934).

turbance, and troops are present to maintain order.[13] Workers on strike may demonstrate, holding processions and public meetings, within the protection of "the rights to meet and discuss and petition," so long as there is no violence or intent to commit acts of violence or breaches of the peace, even though the object of the demonstration is to protest publicly against action taken by the police.[14] Deeply rooted are the rights of the people "to meet in public places to discuss in an open and public manner all questions affecting their substantial welfare and to vent their grievances, to protest against oppression, economic or otherwise, and to petition for the amelioration of their condition, and to discuss the ways and means of attaining that end. . . ."[15] The Supreme Court of Colorado recently upheld as legal the picketing of the governor's mansion by a group which chanted grievances and carried signs, where no profane or offensive language was used, and there was no showing in the record that anyone complained to the police or to anyone else.[16] In the absence of assaults, fighting, or violence, or tumultuous or offensive conduct, the court could find no warrant for a conviction for the offense of "disturbing the peace of others." The court took the view that the right of the community to peace and quiet must be balanced against the constitutional right to appeal to the authorities for a redress of grievances. "It would seem," it observed, "that what the public endures for the sake of sports, it should be able to endure in the assertion of fundamental rights. That is part of the price of our freedoms."[17]

American courts, in contrast with British, do not look with favor upon the view that the police may forbid a public meeting merely because they have reasonable grounds to believe that public disorder will result if the meeting is held, although there are some holdings to the effect that the police do not have to wait until the disorder occurs.[18] Nevertheless, it cannot be

[13] *Neelley* v. *Farr*, 61 Colo. 485, 158 P. 458 (1916).

[14] *State* v. *Butterworth*, 104 N.J.L. 579, 142 A. 57, 58 A.L.R. 744 (1928).

[15] *Ibid.*, at 581, 142 A. at 58.

[16] *Flores* v. *Denver*, 122 Colo. 71, 220 P. 2d 373 (1950).

[17] *Ibid.*, at 78, 220 P. at 376.

[18] See e.g., *Com.* v. *Benjamin*, 10 Pa. D. & C. 775 (1928). This court held that the police are specially qualified by training and experience to know the conditions and anticipate the probable results of a public meeting.

denied that police discretion, under our set of rules, is bound to be very great. A resourceful police chief who is determined to prevent a meeting from being held has many weapons available, such as calling in the building inspectors to find flaws in the building. Police harassment in this area is one of the familiar facts of life.

While the First Amendment guaranty of the right of assembly applies only to the national government, since the late 1920's the Supreme Court has taken the view that it is one of the basic rights of liberty which are protected against invasion by the states under the Due Process Clause of the Fourteenth Amendment. This means, of course, that in the Supreme Court's view the right of assembly is so fundamental as to be essential for any system of ordered liberty. Thus, while the Court sustained a conviction for violation of the California Criminal Syndicalism Act in *Whitney* v. *California*,[19] it proceeded on the assumption, explicitly spelled out, that the rights of assembly and association were within the federally enforceable Due Process Clause of the Fourteenth Amendment. In 1937, in *De Jonge* v. *Oregon*,[20] a unanimous Court ruled that a state statute which punishes participation in a meeting for lawful discussion of public issues, because held under the auspices of the Communist Party, is repugnant to due process. "Peaceable assembly for lawful discussion," Mr. Chief Justice Hughes declared, "cannot be made a crime. The holding of meetings for peaceable political action cannot be proscribed. Those who assist in the conduct of such meetings cannot be branded as criminals on that score." The right to take part in a peaceable assembly is a personal right. Whoever sponsored the meeting, "the defendant was none the less entitled to discuss the public issues of the day and thus in a lawful manner, without incitement to violence or crime, to seek redress of alleged grievances. That was the essence of his guaranteed personal liberty."

Similarly, the Court ruled in 1939, in *Hague* v. *C.I.O.*,[21] and again in 1945, in *Thomas* v. *Collins*,[22] that the right of unions to hold public meetings was protected against improper state

[19] 274 U.S. 357 (1927). See also *Stromberg* v. *California,* 283 U.S. 359 (1931).

[20] 299 U.S. 353.

[21] 307 U.S. 496.   [22] 323 U.S. 516.

interference by the Due Process Clause. In the latter case Mr. Justice Rutledge observed that "It was not by accident or coincidence that the rights to freedom in speech and press were coupled in a single guaranty with the rights of the people peaceably to assemble and to petition for redress of grievances. All these, though not identical, are inseparable. They are cognate rights, . . . and therefore are united in the First Article's assurance." In this case it was decisive that "the assembly was entirely peaceable, and had no other than a wholly lawful purpose." And Mr. Justice Rutledge concluded his opinion with the observation that the right in question "is a national right, federally guaranteed. There is some modicum of freedom of thought, speech and assembly which all citizens of the Republic may exercise throughout its length and breadth, which no State, nor all together, nor the Nation itself, can prohibit, restrain or impede."

MEETINGS IN STREETS AND OTHER PUBLIC PLACES

Since earliest times, meetings have been held in streets, parks, and other public places. Meetings in such places often create serious problems of disorder and breach of the peace. Furthermore, the primary purpose of the streets is passage, and parks are mainly for repose and recreation. Accordingly, American law has long been concerned with the problems created by the holding of meetings in public places.[23] But while street and park meetings are properly subject to regulation, it would be going too far, as a matter of public policy, to forbid them altogether. A short answer to the familiar observation that if one wants to make a speech he ought to "hire a hall" is that halls cost money which the speaker may not have, or halls may not be available, or the right hall may not be had. Furthermore, those who stage street meetings often count on capturing the

[23] See Glenn Abernathy, "Assemblies in Public Streets," *South Carolina Law Quarterly,* V (March, 1953), 384–416; L. Saulson, "Municipal Control of Public Streets and Parks as Affecting Freedom of Speech and Assembly," *Michigan Law Review,* XLIX (June, 1951), 1185–99; Comment, "Public Order and the Right of Assembly in England and the United States: A Comparative Study," *Yale Law Journal,* XLVII (January, 1938), 404–32; Comment, "Municipal Regulation of Free Speech in the Streets and Parks," *Illinois Law Review,* XLVI (July–August, 1951), 489–97.

attention of those who happen to be passing by and bringing to their attention views and facts which might otherwise escape them.

The right to hold a street meeting ends at the point where unlawful assembly and riot begin. In addition, the police may interfere where a breach of the peace or disorderly conduct has occurred. For example, the New York Penal Law says, among other things, that one is guilty of disorderly conduct who "congregates with others on a public street and refuses to move on when ordered by the police," or "by his actions causes a crowd to collect, except when lawfully addressing such a crowd."[24] Convictions have been sustained by the New York courts under this statute over the objection that the right of assembly was interfered with.[25] This right, it is noted, is relative and not absolute in character, and must be exercised with due regard for the public welfare.

Reliance is had, however, principally on municipal ordinances for handling the problems arising from street meetings. Two types of ordinances are available for this purpose, those forbidding obstruction of the streets, and those requiring a permit from some public official or governmental body. There is no doubt at all of the constitutionality of an ordinance which has as its purpose to keep street traffic free from obstruction. Thus in a leading case decided in 1929 by the highest court of Massachusetts, Chief Justice Rugg recognized that the right of peaceable assembly is secured by the state constitution, and as an indubitable and important right is scrupulously protected by the judiciary. Nevertheless, he declared, it "cannot be exercised at times and places and in circumstances in conflict with the enjoyment of other well recognized rights of individuals or the public. . . . The easement of passage for the public acquired by

[24] N.Y. Penal Law, § 722, 3-4.

[25] *People ex rel. Neiman* v. *McWilliams*, 22 N.Y.S. 2d 571 (Mag. Ct. N.Y. City 1940), *reversed on other grounds*, 31 N.Y.S. 2d 37 (1st Dept. 1941); *People* v. *Hussock*, 23 N.Y.S. 2d 520 (Sp. Sess. N.Y. Co. 1940), *certiorari denied*, 312 U.S. 659 (1941); *People ex rel. Whelan* v. *Friedman*, 14 N.Y.S. 2d 389 (Mag. Ct. N.Y. City 1939). In *People* v. *Kieran*, 26 N.Y.S. 2d 291 (Co. Ct. Nassau Co., 1941), which involved a Jehovah's Witnesses' procession of 14 people, the court concluded that the defendants were not guilty of disorderly conduct.

the layout of a highway includes reasonable means of transportation for persons and commodities and of transmission of intelligence. Whatever interferes with the exercise of this easement is a nuisance, even though no inconvenience or delay to public travel actually takes place."[26] Thus the court held it to be immaterial that the defendant had a permit, since it was beyond the ordinance-making power of the city to grant a permit which authorized an obstruction of a public way.

Similarly, it has been held that the policeman is not given arbitrary power where an ordinance authorizes him to break up a meeting on a street if there is an obstruction to traffic.[27] While the police are obliged to act reasonably, it is clear that in protecting traffic from obstruction they have a broad discretion, based on considerations of public safety and convenience in the light of such factors as time, place, and conditions of traffic.[28]

It is important to note, however, that making a speech in a street is not a nuisance per se, for any such rule "is scarcely suited to the genius of our people or to the character of their institutions, and would lead to the repression of many usages of

[26] *Com. v. Surridge*, 265 Mass. 425, 427, 164 N.E. 480, 482, 62 A.L.R. 402 (1929). For similar holdings see *Harwood v. Trembley*, 97 N.J.L. 173, 116 A. 430 (1922); *Barker v. Com.*, 19 Pa. 412 (1852); *Tacoma v. Roe*, 190 Wash. 444, 68 P. 2d 1028 (1937); *Ex parte Bodkin*, 86 Cal. App. 2d 208, 194 P. 2d 588 (1948); *Louisville v. Lougher*, 209 Ky. 299, 272 S.W. 748 (1925); *People v. Pierce*, 85 App. Div. 125, 83 N.Y.S. 79 (3d Dept. 1903). Evidence of obstruction was found to be insufficient by the court in *People v. De Cecca*, 29 N.Y.S. 2d 524 (Sp. Sess. N.Y. Co. 1941), involving a group of Jehovah's Witnesses. In *Wilson v. Eureka City*, 173 U.S. 32 (1899), the Supreme Court upheld an ordinance which provided that no building could be moved on the streets without the written permission of the mayor or president of the city council.

[27] *State v. Sugarman*, 126 Minn. 477, 149 N.W. 466 (1914).

[28] *Burkitt v. Beggans*, 103 N.J. Eq. 7, 142 A. 181 (1928). The court said: "The public streets and highways are not places where any person may claim an unqualified right to be for the purpose of addressing assemblages gathered as audiences; they are intended for passage and traffic and not for assemblage. Sound public policy forbids that courts should interpose by injunctive process to hamper or thwart the power and discretion of the police touching the performance of the duties which the law has cast upon or entrusted to them pertaining to the public weal." *Ibid.* at 10, 142 A. at 182–83.

the people now tolerated as harmless, if not necessary."[29] Similarly, an ordinance forbidding all processions and parades on the streets calculated to attract a crowd is unreasonable, since "a crowd of people is one of the most ordinary incidents of everyday life in any city of considerable size in this country."[30] Many years ago the Kansas Supreme Court declared that it is "an abridgement of the rights of the people" to prohibit all street parades, since

it represses associated effort and action. It discourages united effort to attract public attention, and challenges public examination and criticism of the associated purposes. It discourages unity of feeling and expression on great public questions, economic, religious, and political. It practically destroys these great public demonstrations that are the most natural product of common aims and kindred purposes.[31]

In fact, the courts have taken a more tolerant attitude toward street parades than toward street meetings. It has been suggested that the reasons may be that the early street parade cases generally involved the Salvation Army, whereas the cases dealing with meetings often involved socialists, communists, and other radicals of the left.[32] An additional explanation may be that since municipal authorities have always granted permits to hold street parades freely to lodges, veterans' associations, and fraternal societies, discrimination in denying permits is easily

[29] *Fairbanks* v. *Kerr & Smith*, 70 Pa. 86, 92, 10 Am. Rep. 664, 669 (1872). See also *Anderson* v. *Tedford*, 80 Fla. 376, 85 So. 673, 10 A.L.R. 1481 (1920).

[30] *Anderson* v. *City of Wellington*, 40 Kan. 173, 19 P. 719 (1888). See *In re Gribben*, 5 Okla. 379, 391-92, 47 P. 1074, 1078 (1897): "A city implies a large aggregation of people. The use of its streets contemplates, not quietude and repose, but the noise, bustle and confusion, incident to the transaction of the lawful business of the people and their lawful and harmless amusements and recreations, pleasures and devotions. These are but incidents of a city's life.

"The tendency of American thought and action is towards association for the accomplishment of good purposes; hence, we see a large portion of our people associated in the various organizations for the promotion of public good, the betterment of mankind and the alleviation of its miseries. Every city has its charitable, benevolent, and religious associations, to say nothing of the great political organizations. . . ."

[31] *Ibid.*, at 178, 19 P. at 722.

[32] Comment, *Yale Law Journal*, see note 23, at p. 430.

spotted by the judges, since the fact of discrimination is apt to be quite obvious. Thus some ordinances which were aimed at the Salvation Army were held unconstitutional by the courts because the exemptions extended to other groups proved discrimination.[33]

In addition to ordinances concerned with the obstruction of traffic, the other type of ordinance which has been used to control street meetings and parades has been that which requires the securing of a permit from some official authority. There has never been any doubt of the propriety of an ordinance which requires a prior permit, but there has been a lively debate over the issue concerning the nature and scope of the discretion which the ordinance vests in the licensing authority. In the leading case of *Commonwealth of Massachusetts* v. *Davis*,[34] the Massachusetts court sustained the conviction of a man who made a public address on the Boston Common without a permit from the mayor, contrary to a local ordinance. Speaking for the court, Mr. Justice Holmes said flatly: "For the legislature absolutely or conditionally to forbid public speaking in a highway or public park is no more an infringement of the rights of a member of the public than for the owner of a private house to forbid it in his house." In affirming, the Supreme Court of the United States could see nothing wrong with the fact that under Massachusetts law there is no right to use the Common except in such manner and subject to such regulations as the legislative body may prescribe.[35] Mr. Justice White declared that the Fourteenth Amendment did not destroy the power of the states to enact police regulations as to subjects within their control. On the strength of this sweeping holding, a number of state courts upheld ordinances which gave some administrative official an undefined discretion to grant or deny permits, on the theory that if the official acted unfairly or arbitrarily, such

[33] *Anderson* v. *Wellington*, 40 Kan. 173, 19 P. 719 (1888); *State ex rel. Garrabad* v. *Dering*, 84 Wis. 585, 54 N.W. 1104 (1893): The Salvation Army "in law . . . has the same right, and is subject to the same restrictions, in its public demonstrations, as any secular body or society which uses similar means for drawing attention or creating interest. . . ." 84 Wis. at 591, 54 N.W. at 1106.

[34] 162 Mass. 510, 39 N.E. 113 (1895).

[35] *Davis* v. *Massachusetts*, 167 U.S. 43 (1897).

action could be corrected by the courts.[36] According to this view, even though the ordinance does not say as much, the administrative official must exercise his discretion in a fair and impartial manner. Similarly, ordinances controlling the holding of street processions in order to avoid public annoyance[37] or riot and other public disorder[38] have been sustained over objections centered on the scope of discretionary power involved.

The more recent view of the Supreme Court, however, is that a statute or ordinance which vests an uncontrolled or insufficiently defined discretionary authority in some public official or governmental body to grant or withhold permits is unconstitutional on its face. This principle was established in 1939 in the important case of *Hague* v. *C.I.O.*[39] Five of seven participating Justices joined in holding invalid an ordinance of Jersey City, though they differed as to which provision of the federal Constitution controlled the judgment. The ordinance provided that no public parades or meetings could be conducted on the streets of the city without a prior permit from the Director of Public Safety, and that he could refuse the permit if, after investigation, he believed it was necessary to prevent "riots, disturbances or disorderly assemblage." In this case permits had repeatedly been denied to a labor organization to hold street meetings for the purpose of discussing the newly-enacted National Labor Relations Act. Justices Roberts and Black thought that the ordinance denied one of the privileges and immunities of United States citizenship, secured by Section 1 of the Fourteenth Amendment, whereas Justices Stone and Reed preferred to rest their decision on the Due Process Clause. Mr. Chief Justice Hughes agreed that the right of citizens to meet for the purpose of discussing a national statute was a federal right or privilege, but he also felt that the record did not adequately

[36] *City of Duquesne* v. *Fincke*, 269 Pa. 112, 112 A. 130 (1920); *People ex rel. Doyle* v. *Atwell*, 197 App. Div. 225, 188 N.Y.S. 803 (2d Dept. 1921), *aff'd*, 232 N.Y. 96, 133 N.E. 364, 25 A.L.R. 107 (1921), *writ of error dismissed*, 261 U.S. 590 (1923). See also *City of Bloomington* v. *Richardson*, 38 Ill. App. 60 (3d Dist. 1889).

[37] *City of Chariton* v. *Fitzsimmons*, 87 Iowa 226, 54 N.W. 146 (1893).

[38] *Thomas* v. *Casey*, 121 N.J.L. 185, 1 A. 2d 866 (1938), *aff'd*, 123 N.J.L. 447, 9 A. 2d 294 (1939).

[39] 307 U.S. 496.

23

support a holding on this theory. Accordingly, he went along with those who invoked the Due Process Clause. Mr. Justice McReynolds dissented on the ground that it is beyond the competence of federal courts to interfere by injunction "with the essential rights of the municipality to control its own parks and streets," which are "intimate local affairs." Mr. Justice Butler also dissented, arguing that *Davis* v. *Massachusetts* was controlling.

Whether the ordinance violated the Privileges and Immunities Clause or the Due Process Clause of the Fourteenth Amendment, the majority agreed that it was constitutionally defective. Mr. Justice Roberts argued that the use of the streets for purposes of assembly, "communicating thoughts between citizens, and discussing public questions," is one of the immemorial uses of streets. While he agreed that the use of the streets in this fashion is not absolute, and "must be exercised in subordination to the general comfort and convenience, and in consonance with peace and good order," nevertheless the right must not be abridged or denied in the guise of regulation. Mr. Justice Roberts agreed with the holding of the trial court that the ordinance was void upon its face.

It does not make comfort or convenience in the use of streets or parks the standard of official action. It enables the Director of Safety to refuse a permit on his mere opinion that such refusal will prevent 'riots, disturbances or disorderly assemblage.' It can thus, as the record discloses, be made the instrument of arbitrary suppression of free expression of views. . . . Uncontrolled official suppression of the privilege cannot be made a substitute for the duty to maintain order. . . .[40]

The basic premise on which the decision in *Hague* v. *C.I.O.* rested was reaffirmed and restated in 1951 in *Kunz* v. *New York*.[41] Kunz, a Baptist minister, was convicted and fined $10 for holding a religious meeting on the streets of New York without a permit. He had requested a permit several times, but had been refused without any reason being given. A city ordi-

[40] 307 U.S. at 516.

[41] 340 U.S. 290; see Richard E. Stewart, "Public Speech and Public Order in Britain and the United States," *Vanderbilt Law Review*, XIII (June, 1960), 625–49.

nance made it unlawful to hold public worship meetings on the streets without first obtaining a permit from the police commissioner. The Supreme Court pointed out that the ordinance made no mention of the reasons for which a permit application could be refused, and that under the interpretation of the state courts the police commissioner, an administrative official, was allowed to exercise discretion in denying applications on the basis of his own interpretation of what is deemed to be conduct condemned by the ordinance. Thus, said Mr. Chief Justice Vinson, the ordinance gave an administrative officer discretionary power to control in advance the right of citizens to speak on religious matters on the streets of New York. This he thought was clearly invalid as a prior restraint. While the Court had recognized in *Cox* v. *New Hampshire*[42] that a statute may be enacted which prevents serious interference with the normal usage of streets and parks, the Chief Justice noted that "we have consistently condemned licensing systems which vest in an administrative official discretion to grant or withhold a permit upon broad criteria unrelated to proper regulation of public places."[43] If, as argued by the state, Kunz's previous meetings had caused disorder, there are appropriate public remedies to protect the peace and order of the community. But the issue here is suppression, not punishment. "It is sufficient to say," the Chief Justice concluded, "that New York cannot vest restraining control over the right to speak on religious subjects in an administrative official where there are no appropriate standards to guide his action."[44]

Mr. Justice Jackson alone dissented in this case, at considerable length and with great vigor. He emphasized the fact that Kunz had specialized in making scurrilous attacks upon Catho-

[42] 312 U.S. 569 (1941). This case upheld a statute which required persons using the public streets for a parade or procession to receive a special license from the local authorities. Said Mr. Chief Justice Hughes: "The authority of a municipality to impose regulations in order to assure the safety and convenience of the people in the use of public highways has never been regarded as inconsistent with civil liberties but rather as one of the means of safeguarding the good order upon which they ultimately depend." 312 U.S. at 574. It was emphasized that the state court had construed the statute as not vesting in the licensing board an arbitrary or an unfettered discretion.

[43] 340 U.S. at 294.   [44] 340 U.S. at 295.

lics and Jews, and invited weighing the value of insulting speech against its potentiality for harm. He said that "to blanket hateful and hate-stirring attacks on races and faiths under the protections for freedom of speech may be a noble innovation. On the other hand, it may be a quixotic tilt at windmills which belittles great principles of liberty."[45] He insisted that it made "a world of difference" that Kunz had been speaking in street meetings, since that posed the question whether New York is obliged to place its streets at his service "to hurl insults at the passerby." He thought that this case fell within the "fighting words" doctrine of the Chaplinsky case.[46] Mr. Justice Jackson argued that the Constitution does not prohibit a city from exercising control over its streets by a permit system which takes into account damage to public peace and order, and he insisted that established doctrine dealing with prior restraints upon speech does not apply to street meetings, which have a different impact upon public order. It seemed hypocritical to him for the Court to strike down the ordinance because of lack of standards for administrative action when in his opinion the Justices themselves did not agree upon First Amendment standards.

A number of state courts have taken the view, some even before these recent Supreme Court decisions, that it is unconstitutional to give officials an undefined discretion to grant or withhold permits to hold meetings or processions in the streets.[47] As the highest court of Connecticut once said, it is improper to make the constitutional liberties of the citizen depend upon "the good impulses of a subordinate official entrusted with unlimited discretion," and further, "there can be no reasonable presumption that an unlimited discretion will not be exercised when the ordinance itself reposes an unlimited discretion."[48]

[45] 340 U.S. at 295.

[46] *Chaplinsky* v. *New Hampshire*, 315 U.S. 568 (1942).

[47] See *Matter of Frazee*, 63 Mich. 396, 30 N.W. 72 (1886); *City of Chicago* v. *Trotter*, 136 Ill. 430, 26 N.E. 359 (1891); *Rich* v. *City of Naperville*, 42 Ill. App. 222 (2d Dist. 1891); *In re Gribben*, 5 Okla. 379, 47 P. 1074 (1897); *Anderson* v. *Tedford*, 80 Fla. 376, 85 So. 673, 10 A.L.R. 1481 (1920); *State* v. *Coleman*, 96 Conn. 190, 113 A. 385 (1921); *A.C.L.U.* v. *Town of Cortlandt*, 109 N.Y.S. 2d 165 (Sup. Ct. Westchester Co. 1951).

[48] *State* v. *Coleman*, 96 Conn. 190, 195–96, 113 A. 385, 387 (1921).

Generally speaking, the rules of law which apply to meetings in the streets apply to the holding of meetings in public parks. The New York Court of Appeals held a few years ago that a statute requiring permits for speech-making in public parks was valid on the construction that the Park Commissioner had authority to refuse a permit only to avoid conflicts among meetings and to preserve the parks.[49] Similarly, the highest court of Wisconsin recently ruled that a city ordinance forbidding all religious meetings in the parks was unconstitutional on the ground that this was not regulation, but a prohibition of the right to meet and speak.[50]

The controlling Supreme Court decision on this subject is *Niemotko* v. *Maryland,*[51] decided by a unanimous vote in 1951. The case grew out of the refusal of the Park Commissioner and City Council of Havre de Grace, Maryland, to permit a group of Jehovah's Witnesses to hold Bible-talk meetings in the town park. Though there was no ordinance which spelled out the requirement for a permit, established local custom required a permit from the Commissioner, subject to appeal to the Council. When these Witnesses were refused a permit, they went ahead anyhow and were arrested by the police at the opening of the meeting. They appealed their convictions under the Maryland disorderly conduct statute for which they had been fined $25 each. The Supreme Court took note of the fact that there was no evidence of disorder, threats of violence, riot, or any sort of conduct which could be considered detrimental to the public peace or order, since even the evidence of the police showed that each defendant had conducted himself "in a manner beyond reproach." Furthermore, the Court stressed the fact that it was completely committed to the proposition that a permit requirement is invalid as a prior restraint "in the absence of narrowly drawn, reasonable and definite standards for the officials to follow." Mr. Chief Justice Vinson pointed out that

[49] *People* v. *Hass,* 299 N.Y. 190, 86 N.E. 2d 169 (1949), *appeal dismissed,* 338 U.S. 803 (1949).

[50] *Milwaukee County* v. *Carter,* 258 Wis. 139, 45 N.W. 2d 90 (1950). *Contra: State* v. *Derrickson,* 97 N.H. 91, 81 A. 2d 312 (1951), *aff'd, Poulos* v. *New Hampshire,* 345 U.S. 395 (1953).

[51] 340 U.S. 268.

all the officials had to go on in this case was an "amorphous 'practice'" which vested all authority to grant or withhold permits in the Commissioner and Council. He could find here no standards at all, no narrowly-drawn limitations, "no circumscribing of this absolute power," but only a "limitless discretion." This case illustrated the central issue, since a search of the record failed to discover any valid basis for the refusal of the permit. Apparently the City Council just didn't like Jehovah's Witnesses. The right to the equal protection of the laws, the Chief Justice declared, in the exercise of First and Fourteenth Amendment freedoms, "has a firmer foundation than the whims or personal opinions of a local governing body."

Two years later, however, in *Poulos* v. *New Hampshire*,[52] which also involved the denial of a park permit to a Jehovah's Witness, the Court made it clear that it is constitutional for a city to require a license before one may conduct religious services in a park, where, as interpreted by the state courts, there is "uniform, nondiscriminatory and consistent administration" of the law. Said Mr. Justice Reed: "There is no basis for saying that freedom and order are not compatible. That would be a decision of desperation. Regulation and suppression are not the same, either in purpose or result, and courts of justice can tell the difference."[53] Furthermore, the Court ruled that where under state law the remedy for a wrongful denial of the permit is through appropriate judicial review, however slow and costly this procedure may be, an aggrieved party must follow it and is not free to go ahead with the meeting without a permit. "Delay is unfortunate," said Mr. Justice Reed, "but the expense and annoyance of litigation is a price citizens must pay for life in an orderly society where the rights of the First Amendment have a real and abiding meaning."[54] Speaking in dissent, Justices Douglas and Black took the position that any licensing of free speech is an unconstitutional prior restraint. They declared that "there is no free speech in the sense of the Constitution when permission must be obtained from an official before a speech can be made."[55]

[52] 345 U.S. 395.

[53] 345 U.S. at 408.

[54] 345 U.S. at 409.

[55] 345 U.S. at 426.

One of the thorny problems arising from the exercise of the right of assembly is that of disorder or threatened disorder growing out of the hostility of the audience. In some states the disturbance of a meeting is a statutory crime,[56] and there have been a few cases of conviction for disturbing public meetings.[57] But in most jurisdictions, if a public meeting is held in a private hall, and no permit is required, the police have no right to be present unless there is reasonable ground to believe that a breach of the peace is being committed.[58]

While the disturber of a meeting may be prosecuted for disorderly conduct, the basic problem of audience hostility arises when the police interfere with the speaker or those who are managing the meeting.[59] Clearly an assembly may be halted when a riotous situation has developed and the police are actually unable to control the mob.[60] This limitation is obviously based on practical necessity. On the other hand, it is unthinkable that the right of assembly should depend entirely upon the fact that hostile members of the crowd may threaten to create disorder. There is certainly no constitutional right to disturb a meeting, but there is a constitutional right to hold one. Federal Circuit Judge Sanborn once stated this point emphatically in a Jehovah's Witness case:[61]

[56] See, e.g., N.Y. Penal Code, § 1470: "A person who without authority of law, wilfully disturbs any assembly or meeting, not unlawful in its character, is guilty of a misdemeanor." Wash. Rev. Code, (1956) § 9.27.010, is to the same effect.

[57] *Com.* v. *Porter,* 1 Gray 476 (Mass. 1854); *People* v. *Malone,* 156 App. Div. 10, 141 N.Y.S. 149 (2d Dept. 1913); *Literell* v. *Com.,* 266 Ky. 235, 98 S.W. 2d 909 (1936). Cf. *Pope* v. *State,* 192 Misc. 587, 79 N.Y.S. 2d 466 (Ct. Cl. 1948), *aff'd,* 277 App. Div. 1015, 99 N.Y.S. 2d 1019 (4th Dept. 1950).

[58] See Note, "Right of the Police To Attend Political Meetings," *International Juridical Association Bulletin,* IV (8) (January, 1936), 6–9.

[59] See Henry M. Quillian, Jr., "Soapbox Oratorical Privileges versus Municipal Tranquility," *Georgia Bar Journal,* XIV (November, 1951), 191–200; Note, "Free Speech and the Hostile Audience," *New York University Law Review,* XXVI (July, 1951), 489–505.

[60] *Star Opera Co., Inc.* v. *Hylan,* 109 Misc. 132, 178 N.Y.S. 179 (Sup. Ct. N.Y. Co. 1919).

[61] *Sellers* v. *Johnson,* 163 F. 2d 877, 881 (8th Cir. 1947), *certiorari denied,* 332 U.S. 851 (1948).

The theory that a group of individuals may be deprived of their constitutional rights of assembly, speech and worship if they have become so unpopular with, or offensive to, the people of a community that their presence in a public park to deliver a Bible lecture is likely to result in riot and bloodshed, is interesting but somewhat difficult to accept. Under such a doctrine, unpopular political, racial, and religious groups might find themselves virtually inarticulate. Certainly the fundamental rights to assemble, to speak, and to worship cannot be abridged merely because persons threaten to stage a riot or because peace officers believe or are afraid that breaches of the peace will occur if the rights are exercised.[62]

And Judge Sanborn concluded with the observation that "the only sound way to enforce the law is to arrest and prosecute those who violate the law," meaning those who unlawfully prevent or interfere with the holding of a lawful meeting.

Nevertheless, Judge Sanborn was unwilling to say that the danger of riot will never justify an interference with such rights as the right of assembly, though he also noted that the evidence on which the police may act to find that there is danger to the peace of the community must be something more solid than "unconfirmed rumors, talk and fears." The nature of this particular problem was thoroughly explored by the Justices of the Supreme Court in *Feiner* v. *New York*,[63] which was decided by a six to three vote in 1951. In this case the police had broken up an open-air meeting at a street corner in Syracuse when an onlooker threatened violence if the police did not interfere with the speaker. Feiner seemed to have stirred up some excitement among a crowd of about eighty people by making derogatory remarks about the President, the American Legion, the mayor of Syracuse, and other local officials. When he refused to obey a police order to stop talking he was arrested and convicted of disorderly conduct. Speaking for the six Justices who voted to affirm the conviction, Chief Justice Vinson insisted that this was not a case of "blind condonation by a state court of arbitrary police action." He stressed that

[62] 163 F. 2d at 881.

[63] 340 U.S. 315. For an interesting debate on this decision see Nanette Dembitz, "Free Speech v. Free-for-All," *The Nation*, CLXXIII (July 14, 1951), 29–31, and Vern Countryman, "Freedom for Insulting Speech—A Reply," *Ibid.* (July 21, 1951), pp. 50–52.

Feiner had had a full, fair trial at which the judge, after hearing testimony on both sides, decided that there had been justification for the police to take action to prevent a breach of the peace. Furthermore, this exercise of discretionary power by the police officers was later approved by two appellate courts. All three state courts recognized Feiner's right to hold a street meeting where he did and to make derogatory remarks about public officials and the American Legion. But they also found that in making the arrest the officers had been motivated solely by a proper concern for the preservation of order and protection of the general welfare. The Court must respect, Mr. Chief Justice Vinson declared, "the interest of the community in maintaining peace and order on its streets." He agreed that ordinary murmurings and objections from a hostile audience cannot be sufficient to warrant silencing a speaker, and he declared that he was not unmindful of the danger of giving overly-zealous police officials complete discretion to break up an otherwise lawful public meeting. But this was not that sort of situation, he said. "It is one thing to say that the police cannot be used as an instrument for the suppression of unpopular views, and another to say that, when as here the speaker passes the bounds of argument or persuasion and undertakes incitement to riot, they are powerless to prevent a breach of the peace."[64]

Of course, one of the leading issues of this case was whether Feiner had actually incited to riot. The majority came close to saying that this is a question of fact to be determined by the police officers in the first instance, subject to review in the courts. They seemed to be impressed with the fact that no fewer than three New York courts, the trial court and two appellate courts, had agreed on the factual issues of the existence of a crisis justifying the drastic police action to preserve peace and order. Speaking in dissent, Mr. Justice Douglas could find nothing in the record except that there had been an unsympathetic audience and the threat of one man to haul the speaker from his box. He insisted that where there is this type of threat, it is the duty of the police to protect the speakers, not to silence them. "If they do not receive it and instead the

[64] 340 U.S. at 321.

police throw their weight on the side of those who would break up the meetings, the police become the new censors of speech."[65] Also dissenting, Mr. Justice Black declared that with this decision the Court was taking "a long step toward totalitarian authority." He did not believe that the facts indicated any imminent threat of riot or uncontrollable disorder, and he did not agree that one isolated threat to assault the speaker was evidence of impending disorder. But above all, what concerned Mr. Justice Black was the implication in the majority opinion that the police had no obligation to protect Feiner's right to talk. Of course they have the power to prevent breaches of the peace, but Mr. Justice Black thought that they should first make every reasonable effort to protect the speaker before interfering with him in the name of preserving order, even to the extent of arresting the man who threatened to intervene. It is true that Feiner continued to talk after he was ordered to desist, but, said Mr. Justice Black, "a man making a lawful address is certainly not required to be silent merely because an officer directs it."

Actually, there is no ready and easy solution to the problem of the hostile audience, for on the one hand the state has an incontestable duty to preserve order by controlling mobs, and on the other hand it is unthinkable that the right to hold a public meeting should be determined by the least tolerant people in the community. It has been suggested that various subjective criteria as to both the speaker and the audience should be evaluated in each particular case.[66] Thus, there is a great deal of difference between a speaker whose purpose is to communicate ideas, and one who intends to promote disorder and breaches of the peace. The former is entitled to protection, whereas the latter is prohibitable. Similarly, there are two types of audience, those that are honestly but unjustifiably enraged by the speech, and those which have a preconceived intent to create disturbances. Thus various combinations of circumstances are possible, and "the clearest case for prohibition of the meeting is made out when both the audience and the speaker are motivated by

[65] 340 U.S. at 331.

[66] Note, "Freedom of Speech and Assembly: The Problem of the Hostile Audience," *Columbia Law Review*, XLIX (December, 1949), 1118–24.

a desire for civil strife."[67] On the other hand, if the speaker's desire is to communicate ideas, and the audience is genuinely aroused, the speech should be permissible if the speaker is not responsible for the intolerance of his audience. Finally, the point is worth making that since the right to hold public meetings is both important and constitutionally guaranteed, all factual doubts had better be resolved in favor of the right rather than against it. But in concrete cases the outcome depends upon the facts, and great weight must be given to the judgment of those who, on the spot, have the initial responsibility for making judgments. That is why it is so important that police officers should be well selected and properly trained to understand the nature of the citizen's constitutional rights. Otherwise these rights tend to get crushed under the weight of the presumption in favor of the regularity of official actions.

[67] *Ibid.*, p. 1123.

CHAPTER III

THE FREEDOM
OF ASSOCIATION

THE RIGHT TO ASSOCIATE

The right of Americans freely to associate with whomever they choose is universally recognized as fundamental in a democratic society.[1] But like all rights, this one does not and cannot function in a social and political vacuum, which means that under some circumstances it is legitimate for government to regulate in order to protect other rights. Again, as in the case of regulation generally, governmental measures bearing upon the freedom of association must ultimately pass the judicial test of reasonableness. To take a rather simple example, one of the supreme officers of the Order of Owls once undertook to solicit new members to form a new nest, and was prosecuted for violating a statute which provided that all officers of secret fraternal organizations who solicit dues-paying members must have been elected by chapter delegates. The New York court ruled that this statute was an arbitrary and unreasonable regulation because, since the society was neither illegal nor immoral, no issue of public health, safety, morals, or protection against fraud was involved.[2]

Of course government may forbid criminal, immoral or seditious associations, but the power to regulate may also be exercised under less obvious circumstances. There are all sorts of

[1] See Harold J. Laski, "Freedom of Association," *Encyclopaedia of the Social Sciences*, VI, 447–50 (1931).

[2] *People ex rel. Niger* v. *Van Dell*, 85 Misc. 92, 146 N.Y.S. 992 (Sup. Ct. Erie Co. 1914).

regulations which apply to political organizations in corrupt practices acts, registration of lobbying statutes, and legislation dealing with the distribution of anonymous political circulars. In order to prevent fraud, states are free to require some form of local registration of those who solicit contributions or members. Associations may be required to register in some way with a designated public official in order to permit service of process and to insure some measure of financial responsibility. Furthermore, if the public interest is served thereby, government may go pretty far in forbidding certain types of association which are generally regarded, in the absence of prohibitory legislation, as being quite lawful.

A familiar example is found in the fact that the right of the state to abolish or forbid student membership in fraternities or other secret societies in public institutions is now well-established in American constitutional law. Most of the state cases deal with orders of school boards forbidding high school students to belong to fraternities or other secret organizations, and the courts have invariably sustained such regulations as being reasonable.[3] There has long been a feeling in this country, the Florida court recently observed, that high school fraternities materially interfere with the purposes of public education.[4] The Washington court once found that the evidence sustained the school board's conclusion that the fraternities fostered a clannish spirit of insubordination to lawful school authority, resulting in "much evil to the good order, harmony, discipline, and general welfare of the school," as well as to scholarship.[5] The Massachusetts court concluded that these secret organizations have possibilities of "genuine harm to the reputation of the school and to the studious habits and personal character of the members."[6]

[3] *Isgrig* v. *Srygley*, 210 Ark. 580, 197 S.W. 2d 39 (1946); *Wilson* v. *Abilene Independent School District*, 190 S.W. 2d 406 (Tex. Civ. App. 1945); *Coggins* v. *Board of Education of City of Durham*, 223 N.C. 763, 28 S.E. 2d 527 (1944).

[4] *Satan Fraternity* v. *Board of Public Instruction for Dade County*, 156 Fla. 222, 22 So. 2d 892 (1945).

[5] *Wayland* v. *Board of School Directors*, 43 Wash. 441, 448, 86 P. 642, 644, 7 L.R.A. (N.S.) 352 (1906).

[6] *Antell* v. *Stokes*, 287 Mass. 103, 191 N.E. 407, 134 A.L.R. 1274 (1934), *per* Rugg, C. J.

This question reached the Supreme Court only once, some years ago, in a case which held valid a Mississippi statute prohibiting Greek-letter fraternities, sororities or other secret societies in all of the state's educational institutions, including the University of Mississippi.[7] The Court was unanimous in concluding that the statute violated neither the Due Process nor the Equal Protection Clause of the Fourteenth Amendment, since it found that the statute was a reasonable disciplinary regulation. Mr. Justice McKenna said that whether fraternities are, as alleged by the appellants, a moral and disciplinary force, was for the state itself to determine, but he observed that the state may have thought that membership in the prohibited societies divided the attention of the students, distracting them from that singleness of purpose which the state desires to exist in its public educational institutions. It was not the province of the Supreme Court, Mr. Justice McKenna observed, to annul state statutes by choosing between disputable considerations regarding their wisdom or necessity.

Ever since Queen's Bench took jurisdiction, in 1844, in a case involving expulsion from the Caledonian Society,[8] Anglo-American courts have been willing to take jurisdiction over cases involving suspension or expulsion from a private club. The legal basis for a court's granting relief in such cases is not usually on any property or contract theory, but on the basis of the member's relation to the association.[9] Some courts have allowed damages, but this is an awkward procedure, and the usual remedy is reinstatement or a declaration that the member had been wrongfully expelled. While a few courts have given relief in equity, the customary and preferred remedy is mandamus.[10]

In general, courts follow the line taken by a leading English

[7] *Waugh* v. *Board of Trustees of the University of Mississippi*, 237 U.S. 589 (1915).

[8] *Innes* v. *Wylie* (Q. B. 1844), 1 Car. and K. 257, 174 Eng. Repr. 800.

[9] Zechariah Chafee, Jr., "The Internal Affairs of Associations not for Profit," *Harvard Law Review*, XLIII (May, 1930), 993–1029.

[10] *Lahiff* v. *St. Joseph's Total Abstinence and Benev. Soc.*, 76 Conn. 648, 57 A. 692, 65 L.R.A. 92 (1904); *Mitchell* v. *Jewish Progressive Club*, 253 Ala. 195, 43 So. 2d 529, 20 A.L.R. 2d 339 (1949).

court in 1881 in the landmark case of *Dawkins* v. *Antrobus*.[11] This case involved the expulsion of a member from the Travellers' Club, according to the rules and procedures of the club, for writing a pamphlet reflecting upon the conduct of another member. It was ruled that a court will not interfere with the decision of a club to expel a member under its rules, unless (1) the rules themselves are contrary to natural justice, or (2) the act of expulsion was accomplished in violation of the rules, or (3) there was malice or lack of good faith in the expulsion.

Actually, within the ambit of these three propositions, courts have been willing to intervene for a variety of reasons:[12] where there was a violation of basic principles of justice; where a fair hearing or trial was denied; where proper notice of hearing was not given, or the accusation was insufficient; where an adequate opportunity to defend was denied; where expulsion was in bad faith, or in violation of law, or in violation of the regulations of the association; where there were serious irregularities in the expulsion proceedings; where the expulsory tribunal was not duly constituted; or where a regulation concerned with expulsion was invalid. Courts are especially reluctant to interfere where an expulsion from a church is due to factional trouble or involves purely doctrinal questions, unless property rights are involved,[13] or the expulsion was due to fraud, since "fraud vitiates all transactions."[14] Courts will inquire whether the expulsion was ordered by an authority having the power to take such action.[15] This reluctance of civil courts to get involved in theological dispute is wholly understandable in a country committed to the separation of church and state. Courts are also

[11] 17 Ch. D. 615 (1881). For a lively account of this famous case see Chafee, *op. cit.*, pp. 993-95.

[12] See the analyses in *Blenko* v. *Schmeltz*, 362 Pa. 365, 67 A. 2d 99, 20 A.L.R. 523 (1949); *Mitchell* v. *Jewish Progressive Club*, 253 Ala. 195, 43 So. 2d 529, 20 A.L.R. 2d 339 (1949); *Richards* v. *Morison*, 229 Mass. 458, 118 N.E 868 (1918).

[13] See *Mount Olive Primitive Baptist Church* v. *Patrick*, 252 Ala. 672, 42 So. 2d 617, 20 A.L.R. 2d 417 (1949); *Bouldin* v. *Alexander*, 15 Wall. (U.S.) 131 (1872).

[14] *Hendryx* v. *People's United Church*, 42 Wash. 336, 84 P. 1123, 4 L.R.A. (N.S.) 1154 (1906).

[15] See *Watson* v. *Jones*, 13 Wall. (U.S.) 679 (1871).

slow to intervene in cases involving schools and colleges, where a high value is attached to autonomy, and in cases involving secret societies, where it is too much trouble to learn the ritual. On the other hand, where expulsion may result in very serious consequences, such as the loss of a job or the weakening of a person's professional standing, courts are more willing to take jurisdiction. Such situations arise where a skilled worker has been expelled from his trade union, or a doctor has been dropped by a medical society, or a broker by his stock exchange.

THE RIGHT TO BELONG TO A POLITICAL PARTY

Since the political party is an indispensable instrumentality of democratic government, the right to associate freely with a party of one's choice is equally fundamental. Mr. Chief Justice Warren stated this point with great clarity in 1957:

Our form of government is built on the premise that every citizen shall have the right to engage in political expression and association. This right was enshrined in the First Amendment of the Bill of Rights. Exercise of these basic freedoms in America has traditionally been through the media of political associations. Any interference with the freedom of a party is simultaneously an interference with the freedom of its adherents.[16]

It is interesting to note that there is no direct authorization of political parties in our federal and state constitutions, though parties are mentioned in one way or another in many state constitutions.[17] Actually, the right to form and belong to political parties is a by-product of many constitutional guarantees, such as the rights of petition and assembly, the rights of free speech and free press, and the right to vote. Courts also take the view that the inherent right of the people to form political parties is a necessary incident of free government. Thus the

[16] *Sweezy* v. *New Hampshire*, 354 U.S. 234, 250 (1957). For an eloquent appreciation of the indispensable role of political parties in the American democracy see Elihu Root, *The Citizen's Part in Government* (New York: Scribner's, 1907), especially chap. ii.

[17] See Joseph R. Starr, "The Legal Status of American Political Parties," *American Political Science Review*, XXXIV (June, 1940), 439–55 (August, 1940), 685–99.

law recognizes a basic right to form political parties. The highest court of California said many years ago:

No one can be so ignorant as not to appreciate the value, indeed, the necessity, of opposing political parties in a government such as ours. No one, it would seem, can be so thoughtless as not to realize that government by the people is a progressive institution which seeks to give expression and effect to the wisest and best ideas of its members. No statement is needed in the declaration of rights to the effect that electors holding certain political principles in common may freely assemble, organize themselves into a political party, and use all legitimate means to carry their principles of government into active operation through the suffrages of their fellows. Such a right is fundamental. It is inherent in the very form and substance of our government, and needs no expression in its constitution.[18]

It follows from all this that our courts generally hold to the view that political parties are not the creatures of government,[19] and this being so, that they have the right to govern themselves. In the absence of statutory regulation, they have an inherent right to manage their own affairs.[20] They may organize themselves by electing officers and committees. Party committees

18 *Britton v. Board of Election Commissioners of San Francisco*, 129 Cal. 337, 344, 61 P. 1115, 1117 (1900). See also *Ex parte Wilson*, 7 Okla. Cr. 610, 125 P. 739 (1912); *Davidson v. Hanson*, 87 Minn. 211, 91 N.W. 1124, 92 N.W. 93, 95 (1902): "The right to agitate and organize political parties is inherent, and secured by the constitution . . ."; *Sarlls v. State ex rel. Trimble*, 210 Ind. 88, 166 N.E. 270 (1929): "The people have an inalienable right to organize and operate political parties. . . ."

19 See *Bell v. Hill*, 123 Tex. 531, 534, 74 S.W. 2d 113, 114 (1934): A political party is "a *voluntary association*, an association formed of the free will and unrestrained choice of those who compose it. No man is compelled by law to become a member of a political party; or, after having become such, to remain a member. He may join such a party for whatever reason seems good to him, and may quit the party for any cause, good, bad, or indifferent, or without cause. A political party is the creation of free men, acting according to their own wisdom, and in no sense whatever the creation of any department of the government."

20 Cf. *Brown v. Costen*, 176 N.C. 63, 96 S.E. 659 (1918), holding that in the absence of statute, a court of equity has no power to interfere with political parties in the choice of candidates, nor to regulate the methods and agencies by which they are selected. See G. Theodore Mitau, "Judicial Determination of Political Party Organizational Autonomy," *Minnesota Law Review*, XLII (December, 1957), 245–68.

have the right to judge the qualifications of their own members, fix the site for conventions, and fill vacancies in the slate of candidates caused by death or withdrawal. A party has the right to adopt and amend its constitution and by-laws.[21] Nevertheless, it is equally incontestable that political parties are subject to reasonable regulation by government, and almost all states have fairly substantial bodies of legislation on the subject. Thus, most states define parties in terms of numerical strength, and their authority to do so has often been affirmed by the courts.[22] Furthermore, the nomination of candidates is now controlled by detailed legislation. Nevertheless, the courts will hold legislation which is regulatory of political parties to be unconstitutional if arbitrary, discriminatory, or unreasonable, just as they have the power so to rule with regard to most types of regulatory enactments.[23]

Many states have in recent years taken to barring "Un-American" parties from the ballot.[24] One type of statute requires each party to file an affidavit with some state official affirming that it does not advocate seditious doctrines and is not affiliated with an organization that does.[25] Another type of statute is one which excludes the Communist Party by name from the ballot.[26] A few state appellate courts have upheld the

[21] See Starr, *op. cit.*, at pp. 448–52.

[22] See *State ex rel. McGrael v. Phelps*, 144 Wis. 1, 128 N.W. 1041 (1910); *Progressive Party v. Flynn*, 400 Ill. 102, 79 N.E. 2d 516 (1948).

[23] See *Morrow v. Wipf*, 22 S.D. 146, 158, 115 N.W. 1121, 1126 (1908).

[24] See Harry F. Ward, "The Communist Party and the Ballot," *Bill of Rights Review*, I (Summer, 1941), 286–92; Walter Gellhorn, ed., *The States and Subversion* (Ithaca, N.Y.: Cornell University Press, 1952), pp. 404–5; Gordon Jaynes, "The Washington Subversive Activities Act: Its Restriction on Access to the Election Process," *Washington Law Review*, XXIX (February, 1954), 63–72; Warren P. Hill, "A Critique of Recent Ohio Anti-Subversive Legislation," *Ohio State Law Journal*, XIV (Autumn, 1953), 439–93.

[25] See Del. Code Anno. tit. 15, § 4101 (1953); Ind. Stat. Anno., § 29–3812 (Burns, 1949); Ohio Rev. Code Anno., § 3517.07 (Page, 1954); Pa. Stat. Anno., tit. 25, §§ 2831, 2936 (Supp. 1958); Tenn. Code Anno., § 2–1203 (1955); Tex. Civ. Stat., Election Code, Art. 6.02 (Vernon, 1952); Wash. Rev. Code, § 9–81–100 (1956).

[26] See Ark. Stat. Anno., §§ 3–1604, 5 (1956); Cal. Election Code, § 2540.9 (1953); Wyo. Stat. Anno., § 31–1404 (1945); Okla. Stat., tit. 26, §§ 6.1–2

constitutionality of this sort of legislation,[27] though the Ohio court has stressed that while a state may bar a party which advocated violent overthrow of government from a place on the ballot, a finding to this effect must be supported by substantial evidence.[28] A number of rulings, however, have gone the other way. The California statute which in effect denied recognition as a political party to the Communist Party was held unconstitutional in 1942 by the state supreme court as a legislative infringement on the constitutional right to vote.[29] The court also ruled that while the legislature may deny any party advocating the forceful overthrow of the government a place on the ballot, it is not within its power to determine that a particular party advocates the doctrine in question. The supreme court of Washington has refused to permit the Secretary of State of Washington to bar the Communist Party from the ballot without statutory authorization to do so.[30] In 1950 the New Jersey courts held unconstitutional a statute which required all candidates for state office to take a special oath swearing to non-belief and non-membership in subversive organizations on the ground that the legislature could not alter the requirements for public office spelled out in the state constitution.[31] On the other hand, in 1951 the Supreme Court sustained the validity of a Maryland law which denied a place on the ballot for a municipal election to a candidate who refused to sign an oath that he was not knowingly a member of an organi-

---

(1951); Ill. Stat. Anno., § 29.3812 (Burns, 1949); Tex. Civ. Stat., Election Code, Art. 6.03 (Vernon, 1952); Wis. Stat., § 685 (1955).

27 *Field* v. *Hall*, 201 Ark. 77, 143 S.W. 2d 567 (1940); *State ex rel. Berry* v. *Hummel*, 42 Ohio Law Abs. 40, 59 N.E. 2d 238 (1944); *Huntamer* v. *Coe*, 40 Wash. 2d 767, 246 P. 2d 489 (1952).

28 *State ex rel. Beck* v. *Hummel*, 150 Ohio St. 127, 80 N.E. 2d 899 (1948).

29 *Communist Party* v. *Peek*, 20 Cal. 2d 536, 127 P. 2d 889 (1942). See Note, "May the States, by Statute, Bar Subversive Groups from the Ballot?" *Notre Dame Lawyer*, XXV (Winter, 1950), 319–29. See also *Feinglass* v. *Reinecke*, 48 F. Supp. 438 (N.D. Ill. 1942).

30 *Washington ex rel. Huff* v. *Reeves*, 5 Wash. 2d 637, 106 P. 2d 729, 130 A.L.R. 1465 (1940).

31 *Imbrie* v. *Marsh*, 5 N.J. Super. 239, 68 A. 2d 761 (1949), *aff'd*, 3 N.J. 578, 71 A. 2d 352, 18 A.L.R. 2d 241 (1950). *Contra: Huntamer* v. *Coe*, 40 Wash. 2d 767, 246 Pac. 2d 489 (1952).

zation which has engaged in any attempt to overthrow the government by force or violence.[32] The Court stressed the fact of *knowing* membership in a subversive organization.

THE RIGHT TO JOIN A TRADE UNION

It is well known that at the common law trade unions were treated as illegal combinations or conspiracies in restraint of trade contrary to the public interest. Such was the decision of the Mayor's Court of Philadelphia in the first American labor case, the Philadelphia Cordwainers' case of 1806.[33] Of course, the Cordwainers' case did not stand alone in this period of our history.[34] Beginning with the landmark decision in 1842 of Chief Justice Shaw in *Commonwealth* v. *Hunt*,[35] however, American courts gradually abandoned the common-law doctrine of criminal conspiracy as a weapon for the suppression of labor unions, and statutes were adopted by legislative bodies to protect the right of workers to organize. Thus Congress declared in 1935, in the National Labor Relations (Wagner) Act,[36] that it was the policy of the United States to encourage

[32] *Gerende* v. *Board of Supervisors of Elections of Baltimore*, 341 U.S. 56 (1951).

[33] For the text see John R. Commons and Eugene Gilmore, *A Documentary History of American Industrial Society* (Cleveland: Arthur H. Clark Co., 1910), III, 61–385. For an excellent analysis of the Cordwainers' Case see Walter Nelles, "The First American Labor Case," *Yale Law Journal*, XLI (December, 1931), 165–200. See also Foster R. Dulles, *Labor in America* (New York: Thomas Y. Crowell, 1949), p. 30; Charles O. Gregory, *Labor and the Law* (2d ed.; New York: W. W. Norton & Co., 1958), chap. i.

[34] See *People* v. *Melvin*, 2 Wheller Cr. Cas. 262 (N.Y. 1810); Pittsburg Cordwainers' Case (1815), Commons and Gilmore, *op. cit.*, IV, 15–87; *People* v. *Fisher*, 14 Wend. 10 (N.Y. 1835). *State* v. *Donaldson*, 32 N.J.L. 151 (1867) was one of the last of these cases.

[35] 45 Mass. (4 Metc.) 111 (1842). See Walter Nelles, "Commonwealth v. Hunt," *Columbia Law Review*, XXXII (November, 1932), 1128–69.

[36] Act of July 5, 1935, ch. 372, § 1, 49 Stat. 449, § 1. For the forerunner of this concept see the National Industrial Recovery Act of 1933, 48 Stat. 195, § 7(a). The Labor-Management Relations (Taft-Hartley) Act of 1947, 61 Stat. 136, § 101, 29 U.S.C. § 151 (1958) opens with a reaffirmation of the declaration of the Wagner Act that workers are entitled to "full freedom of association, self-organization, and designation of representatives of their own choosing. . . ."

"the practice and procedure of collective bargaining" and to protect "the exercise by workers of full freedom of association, self-organization, and designation of representatives of their own choosing. . . ." In sustaining the statute over constitutional objections, Mr. Chief Justice Hughes declared that the right of workers to self-organization to bargain collectively through representatives of their own choosing was a "fundamental right. Employees have as clear a right to organize and select their representatives for lawful purposes as the respondent has to organize its business and select its own officers and agents."[37] He went on to say that long ago the Court had explained the underlying reasons for labor organizations.

We said that they were organized out of the necessities of the situation; that a single employee was helpless in dealing with an employer; that he was dependent ordinarily on his daily wage for the maintenance of himself and family; that if the employer refused to pay him the wages that he thought fair, he was nevertheless unable to leave the employ and resist arbitrary and unfair treatment; that union was essential to give laborers opportunity to deal on an equality with their employer.[38]

Some years ago a town in Florida adopted an ordinance which in effect made it unlawful to organize or attempt to organize any labor union within the town, and prohibited the solicitation of union memberships on the streets or in any public place. The Supreme Court of Florida held this ordinance unconstitutional as an abridgment of a fundmental right.[39] The

[37] *National Labor Relations Board* v. *Jones & Laughlin Steel Corp.*, 301 U.S. 1, 33 (1937).

[38] *Ibid.* This is a paraphrase of a classic statement of the right of workers to organize trade unions written by Mr. Chief Justice Taft in *American Steel Foundries* v. *Tri-City Central Trades Council*, 257 U.S. 184, 209 (1921). See also *Brown* v. *Stoerkel and Gregory*, 74 Mich. 269, 276, 41 N.W. 921, 923 (1889), where, speaking of an unincorporated local of the old Knights of Labor, the court said: "It was purely a benevolent and social organization, having also in view the protection, benefit, and welfare of its members in their various employments. It must now be considered as well settled that persons have a right to enter into such associations, and to bind themselves as to their membership and rights in such societies. . . ."

[39] *Pittman* v. *Nix*, 152 Fla. 378, 11 So. 2d 791 (1943). The court relied heavily upon *Paramount Enterprises, Inc.* v. *Mitchell*, 104 Fla. 407, 140 So. 328 (1932), which affirmed a denial of an injunction to restrain union picketing.

court said it was not permissible to impair "the well settled legal right of employed workers to organise labor unions and to use their powers of persuasion to induce others to join, so long as no fraud or coercion is resorted to."

Trade unions have generally had the status of unincorporated associations, although under the laws of many states incorporation is available to them. Before the adoption of the Labor-Management Relations Act of 1947 there was some pressure to compel unions to incorporate because of a desire to hold them more effectively liable for wrongful acts. Apprehensions on this score were eliminated by Sections 301 and 303 of the 1947 statute, which make it perfectly clear that unincorporated unions may be sued. On the other hand, it is clear that in many circumstances a union may sue on behalf of its members since "there is a direct community of interest between it and its members. . . ."[40] The Colorado legislature adopted a Labor Peace Act in 1943 which required all unions to incorporate, but the following year the Supreme Court of the state held this provision unconstitutional as going beyond the limits of permissible regulation.[41] It held that the statute unconstitutionally denied unincorporated unions the right to assemble and function, and that the guaranty of the right of assembly was not restricted to the literal right of meeting together to petition the government for a redress of grievances.

No one has ever pretended, however, that trade unions are altogether immune from proper statutory regulation, although the Supreme Court will go far in construing an act of Congress to avoid imputing to that body any intention of interfering with a union's exercise of such constitutional rights as that of publishing its views on political matters.[42] Similarly, since union

[40] *Brotherhood of Stationary Engineers* v. *St. Louis*, 212 S.W. 2d 454 (Mo. App. 1948). An association has no standing to sue in court to enjoin the enforcement of a statute if it is not itself subject to the challenged enactment. *Northwestern Pennsylvania Phonograph Assn.* v. *Meadville*, 359 Pa. 549, 59 A. 2d 907, 2 A.L.R. 2d 913 (1958); *Georgia Music Operators Assn.* v. *Atlanta*, 183 Ga. 794, 190 S.E. 32 (1937).

[41] *American Federation of Labor* v. *Reilly*, 113 Colo. 90, 155 P. 2d 145, 160 A.L.R. 873 (1944).

[42] *United States* v. *C.I.O.*, 335 U.S. 106 (1948). Coming directly to the point in a concurring opinion, Mr. Justice Rutledge said, at p. 143: "The

44

meetings are entitled to privacy, a federal court once enjoined the members of the state police from attending union meetings, because it was found that their presence had the actual effect of active interference.[43] The court asserted that the right to speak freely and assemble peaceably for any lawful purpose without the interference of officials is not limited to assembling and speaking in a public forum. Equally protected by the Constitution is "the freedom and liberty to express ourselves privately and to hold private assemblies for lawful purposes and in a lawful manner without governmental interference or hindrance. . . ."[44] Similarly, the Supreme Court ruled in 1945 that a state may not require labor organizers to register, since this is an improper restraint upon the rights of free speech and peaceable assembly.[45]

But unions are subject to all sorts of limitations. While peaceful persuasion and picketing by union members are lawful,[46] picketing in a context of violence[47] or for unlawful objectives[48] may be forbidden, as well as unlawful or riotous assembly.[49] Since there is no constitutional right to injure someone who is not a party to the labor dispute, statutes making secondary boycotts illegal have been sustained by the courts.[50] States are at

---

expression of bloc sentiment is and always has been an integral part of our democratic electoral and legislative processes. They could hardly go on without it."

[43] *Local 309, United Furniture Workers* v. *Gates,* 75 F. Supp. 620 (N.D. Ind. 1948).

[44] *Ibid.,* at 624.   [45] *Thomas* v. *Collins,* 323 U.S. 516 (1945).

[46] *Thornhill* v. *Alabama,* 310 U.S. 88 (1940); *Carlson* v. *California,* 310 U.S. 106 (1940).

[47] *Milk Wagon Drivers Union* v. *Meadowmoor Co.,* 312 U.S. 287 (1941).

[48] *Giboney* v. *Empire Storage & Ice Co.,* 336 U.S. 490 (1949); *Building Service Union* v. *Gazzam,* 339 U.S. 532 (1950); *Hughes* v. *Superior Court,* 339 U.S. 460 (1950); *Teamsters Union* v. *Hanke,* 339 U.S. 470 (1950).

[49] *Lair* v. *State,* 316 P. 2d 225 (Okla. Cr. 1957); *State* v. *Johnson,* 89 Iowa 594, 57 N.W. 302 (1894).

[50] See *Carpenters & Joiners Union* v. *Ritter's Cafe,* 315 U.S. 722 (1942); *State* v. *Casselman,* 69 Ida. 237, 205 P. 2d 1131 (1949), *cert. denied,* 338 U.S. 900 (1949). The state may also forbid a union "slow-down" as an unfair labor practice. *United Auto Workers* v. *Wisconsin Employment Relations Board,* 336 U.S. 245 (1949).

liberty to forbid trade unions to deny membership or otherwise discriminate by reason of race, creed, or color.[51] State legislation outlawing the closed shop has also been sustained on the theory that the state is as free to safeguard the opportunity of non-union workers to get and hold jobs as it is to legislate in favor of union membership.[52] However, state policy must give way in such areas of federal interest as the railroad field, which is covered by a federal statute[53] permitting union shop agreements.[54] Congress has great latitude in regulating the labor relations of interstate industries, and the choice of the union shop as a stabilizing force is an allowable one. Speaking for a unanimous Court, Mr. Justice Douglas observed that "one would have to be blind to history to assert that trade unionism did not enhance and strengthen the right to work."[55] But the Taft-Hartley Act of 1947 validly forbids the unions to do a great many things which are described by the statute as unfair labor practices.

Membership in a trade union is normally a valuable right, the denial of which is subject to judicial review.[56] To be sure, unions are free to expel members or officers for a variety of reasons, such as publicly criticizing the officers on the board of the union contrary to the union constitution or without permission,[57] or refusing to pay a special political assessment levied

[51] *Railway Mail Assoc.* v. *Corsi*, 326 U.S. 88 (1945).

[52] *Lincoln Union* v. *Northwestern Iron & Metal Co.*, 335 U.S. 525 (1949); *American Federation of Labor* v. *American Sash and Door Co.*, 335 U.S. 538 (1949). See G. Rose, "Legal Protection of Voluntary Union Membership," *Labor Law Journal*, XI (May, 1960), 385–406.

[53] Railway Labor Act, 64 Stat. 1238, § 2, Eleventh, 45 U.S.C. § 152, Eleventh (1958).

[54] *Railway Employes' Dept., A.F. of L.* v. *Hanson*, 351 U.S. 225 (1956).

[55] *Ibid.,* at 235.

[56] See Jerre S. Williams, "The Political Liberties of Labor Union Members," *Texas Law Review*, XXXII (October, 1954), 826–38; Note, "Constitutional Right to Membership in a Labor Union," *Journal of Public Law*, VIII (Fall, 1959), 580–601.

[57] *Dame* v. *LeFevre*, 251 Wis. 146, 28 N.W. 2d 349 (1947); *Elfer* v. *Marine Engineers Beneficial Assoc.*, 179 La. 383, 154 So. 32 (1934); *Love* v. *Grand International Division of the Brotherhood of Locomotive Engineers*, 139 Ark. 375, 215 S.W. 602 (1919). In *Pfoh* v. *Whitney*, 62 N.E. 2d

to finance a fight against a state anti-union security law.[58] But courts are quite competent to annul expulsions from unions, and have often done so on various grounds, such as lack of hearing,[59] faulty charge,[60] procedural failures,[61] or invasion of free speech.[62] It has been pointed out that "numerous cases hold that where the expulsion or suspension of a member of the Union affects the individual's property rights, a court of equity will award relief to a member wrongfully expelled or suspended from the Union by decreeing his re-instatement, at least where a resort to the internal remedies within the union would be futile, illusory or useless, or would not accord to the members in question substantial or practical justice."[63]

There has been a great deal of public concern in recent years with issues regarding the uses of trade union power, as the labor movement becomes more and more institutionalized and bureaucratized. In particular, questions have been raised about the rights of rank-and-file members within the unions.[64] Following

744 (Ohio App. 1945), a member was expelled for circulating a political campaign letter to a number of lodges, without the approval of the president, as required by the union constitution. In *Hall* v. *Morrin*, 293 S.W. 435 (Mo. App. 1927), a member was suspended for five years for bringing a law suit claiming that an international officer had wantonly declared a local election void.

[58] *De-Mille* v. *American Federation of Radio Artists*, 17 A.C.A. 480, 175 P. 2d 851 (Cal. App. 1946), aff'd, 31 Cal. 2d 139, 187 P. 2d 769 (1947), *cert. denied*, 333 U.S. 876 (1948).

[59] *O'Brien* v. *Papas*, 49 N.Y.S. 2d 521 (Sup. Ct. King Co. 1944).

[60] *Johnson* v. *International of United Brotherhood*, 52 Nev. 400, 288 P. 170 (1930).

[61] *Polin* v. *Kaplan*, 257 N.Y. 277, 177 N.E. 833 (1931).

[62] *Crossen* v. *Duffy*, 103 N.E. 2d 769 (Ohio App. 1951). In this case members had been fined for pamphleteering in a union election in opposition to the incumbents.

[63] *Ibid.*, at 779. See 168 A.L.R. 1462.

[64] See James S. Coleman, Seymour M. Lipset and Martin A. Trow, *Union Democracy* (Glencoe, Illinois: Free Press, 1956); Roger N. Baldwin, "Union Administration and Civil Liberties," *Annals of the American Academy*, CCXLVIII (November, 1946), 54–61; A. W. Blumrosen, "Group Interests in Labor Law," *Rutgers Law Review*, XIII (Spring, 1959), 432–84.

prolonged hearings by its committees, especially the McClellan Committee, Congress adopted the Labor-Management Reporting and Disclosure Act of 1959,[65] which recited that there had been "a number of instances of breach of trust, corruption, disregard of the rights of individual employees, and other failures to observe high standards of responsibility and ethical conduct. . . ."[66] Title I of this comprehensive statute is entitled, "Bill of Rights of Members of Labor Organizations." It is declared that "every member of a labor organization shall have equal rights and privileges within such organization to nominate candidates, to vote in elections or referendums of the labor organization, to attend membership meetings, and to participate in the deliberations and voting upon the business of such meetings, subject to reasonable rules and regulations in such organization's constitution and bylaws."[67] It is also provided that "every member of any labor organization shall have the right to meet and assemble freely with other members; and to express any views, arguments, or opinions; and to express at meetings of the labor organization his views, upon candidates in an election of the labor organization or upon any business properly before the meeting, subject to the organization's established and reasonable rules. . . ."[68] The statute then spells out certain safeguards in the levying of dues, initiation fees and assessments,[69] and protects the member's right to sue in court or in a proceeding before administrative agencies.[70] Finally, it is stipulated that no member may be fined, suspended, expelled, or otherwise disciplined, except for nonpayment of dues, "unless such member has been (A) served with written specific charges; (B) given a reasonable time to prepare his defense; (C) afforded a full and fair hearing."[71] Whether justified or not, these provisions add up to an extraordinary amount of governmental intervention into the affairs of voluntary associations.

[65] 73 Stat. 519 (1959), 29 U.S.C.A. 401 *et seq.* (1960). See the symposium on this statute in the *Georgetown Law Journal,* XLVIII (Winter, 1959), 205–429.

[66] *Ibid.,* § 2 (b).

[67] *Ibid.,* § 101 (a) (1).

[68] *Ibid.,* § 101 (a) (2).

[69] *Ibid.,* § 101 (a) (3).

[70] *Ibid.,* § 101 (a) (4).

[71] *Ibid.,* § 101 (a) (5).

It remains to be noted that while as a general proposition it may be asserted that workers in this country have a right to join trade unions, limitations on this right have been recognized in the field of public employment. While the general rule, in the absence of a statute forbidding it, is that public employees may organize, a notable exception is that policemen are usually forbidden to belong to unions, and courts have invariably upheld such a prohibition.[72] The rationale behind this rule is that policemen have very special functions to perform which require undivided allegiance to the public. These men are paid by all and must act without any favoritism in the discharge of their important duties. It is also stressed that the police force is a semimilitary organization, for which order, discipline, and authority are absolutely essential. The fear is expressed that membership in a union might cause friction and dissension to the prejudice of law enforcement. For about the same reasons American courts regard firemen as constituting a class apart who may be denied the privilege of belonging to trade unions.[73]

Except for such special classes as policemen and firemen, city and state employees are generally conceded the right to join unions,[74] though a city does not act unlawfully if it prohibits any of its employees from becoming members of a labor union.[75] Ever since the Lloyd-LaFollette Act of 1912[76] confirmed the right of postal workers to organize unions, the Civil Service Act has recognized that federal employees may organ-

[72] *City of Jackson* v. *McLeod*, 199 Miss. 676, 24 So. 2d 319 (1946), *cert. denied*, 328 U.S. 863 (1946); *King* v. *Priest*, 357 Mo. 68, 206 S.W. 2d 547 (1947), *appeal dismissed*, 333 U.S. 852 (1948); *State Lodge of Michigan* v. *Detroit*, 318 Mich. 182, 27 N.W. 2d 612 (1947), *cert. denied*, 332 U.S. 818 (1947); *Fraternal Order of Police* v. *Lansing Board of P. & F. Comrs.*, 306 Mich. 68, 10 N.W. 2d 310 (1943), *cert. denied*, 321 U.S. 784 (1944); *Perez* v. *Brd. of Police Comrs.*, 78 Cal. App. 2d 638, 178 P. 2d 537 (1947); *Goodwin* v. *Oklahoma City*, 199 Okla. 26, 182 P. 2d 762 (1947).

[73] *Carter* v. *Thompson*, 164 Va. 312, 180 S.E. 410 (1935); *Hutchinson* v. *Magee*, 278 Pa. 119, 122 A. 234 (1923); *McNatt* v. *Lawther*, 223 S.W. 503 (Tex. Civ. App. 1920); *San Antonio Fire Fighters' Local Union No. 84* v. *Bell*, 223 S.W. 506 (Tex. Civ. App. 1920).

[74] See *Hagen* v. *Picard*, 171 Misc. 475, 12 N.Y.S. 2d 873 (Sup. Ct. Albany Co. 1939), *aff'd*, 258 App. Div. 771, 14 N.Y.S. 2d 706 (3d Dept. 1939).

[75] *C.I.O.* v. *City of Dallas*, 198 S.W. 2d 143 (Tex. Civ. App. 1946).

[76] 37 Stat. 539, § 6 (1912).

ize.[77] But while most governmental employees in the United States are free to join unions, they are not permitted to strike or picket.[78] As Governor Calvin Coolidge of Massachusetts declared so succinctly in connection with the famous Boston police strike, "There is no right to strike against the public safety by anybody, any time, anywhere."[79] Thus, the Taft-Hartley Act of 1947 provides that "it shall be unlawful for any individual employed by the United States or any agency thereof including wholly owned Government corporations to participate in any strike."[80] The penalty for striking is immediate discharge, forfeiture of civil service status, and ineligibility for re-employment for three years. In addition, Congress has stipulated that no money shall be payable to anyone who strikes against the United States or who belongs to an organization of government workers which asserts that right.[81] Many states now have no-strike statutes of this sort,[82] and it is well-established in state decisional law that state governmental employees may not engage in strikes.[83]

In addition, for reasons of public policy, governments in the United States, with a few exceptions, do not and may not enter into collective bargaining agreements with unions of public employees.[84] Thus, federal labor relations statutes, such as the

[77] 37 Stat. 555 (1912), as amended, 62 Stat. 354 (1948), 5 U.S.C. § 652 (c) (1952).

[78] Strikes against government have occurred. See David Ziskind, *One Thousand Strikes of Government Employees* (New York: Columbia University Press, 1940). See also Sterling D. Spero, *Government As Employer* (New York: Remsen Press, 1948); John H. Leek, *Government and Labor in the United States* (New York: Rinehart, 1952), chap. xv.

[79] See William Allen White, *A Puritan in Babylon* (New York: Macmillan, 1938), p. 166.

[80] 61 Stat. 136, § 305 (1947), 29 U.S.C. § 145 (1952).

[81] 60 Stat. 910, 918, § 301 (1946).

[82] See, e.g., New York Laws, 1947, chap. 391.

[83] See *City of Los Angeles* v. *Los Angeles Bldg. & Constr. Trades Council*, 94 Cal. App. 2d 36, 210 P. 2d 305 (1949); *Broadwater* v. *Otto*, 370 Pa. 611, 88 A. 2d 878 (1952); *Goodfellow* v. *Detroit Civil Service Commission*, 312 Mich. 226, 20 N.W. 2d 170 (1945).

[84] See Isadore Vogel, "What about the Rights of the Public Employee?" *Labor Law Journal*, I (May, 1950), 604-18. The controlling statute, 48

Labor-Management Relations Act of 1947,[85] the Fair Labor Standards Act of 1938,[86] and the War Labor Disputes Act of 1943,[87] exclude public employment from their operations. Accordingly, the National War Labor Board held in 1942 that it had no jurisdiction over unions of public employees in several large cities. Dean Wayne Morse, the public member of the Board, declared that "the well established doctrines in American law pertaining to the sovereign rights of state and local governments, clearly exclude such disputes from the jurisdiction and powers of the Board."[88] It follows that while most public employees may organize, their organizations have limited powers and are not conceded to have normal collective bargaining rights.[89] As the Missouri supreme court explained a few years ago, collective bargaining is inappropriate because the wages and hours of public employees are fixed by statute or ordinance, and cannot be the subject of bargaining.[90] It noted that "legislative discretion cannot be lawfully bargained away and no citizen or group of citizens have any right to a contract for any legislation or to prevent legislation." It is wholly impermissible to have government by private agreement. "Under our form of government," it declared, "public office or employment never has been and cannot become a

---

Stat. 58, § 3 (1933), 16 U.S.C. 831 (b) (1952), permits TVA to bargain with employee unions, and there is real bargaining in TVA.

[85] 61 Stat. 137, § 101 (1947) 29 U.S.C., § 152 (2) (1952).

[86] 52 Stat. 1060, § 3 (1938), 29 U.S.C., § 203 (d) (1952).

[87] 57 Stat. 163, § 2 (1943), 50 U.S.C., §§ 1501, 1502 (d) (1952).

[88] Ludwig Teller, *Labor Disputes and Collective Bargaining* (New York: Baker Voorhis & Co.), I (1947 Supp.), 116.

[89] See *National Council of Railway Patrolman's Union* v. *Sealy*, 56 F. Supp. 720 (S.D. Tex. 1944); *State* v. *Brotherhood of R. Trainmen*, 37 Cal. 2d 412, 232 P.2d 857 (1951), *cert. denied*, 342 U.S. 876 (1951); *Nutter* v. *Santa Monica*, 74 Cal. App. 2d 292, 168 P. 2d 741 (1946); *Miami Water Works Local No. 654* v. *Miami*, 157 Fla. 445, 26 So. 2d 194, 165 A.L.R. 967 (1946); *Mugford* v. *Mayor and City Council of Baltimore*, 185 Md. 266, 44 A. 2d 745, 165 A.L.R. 967 (1945); *Cleveland* v. *Division 268*, 30 Ohio Ops. 395 (Com. Pl. Cuyahoga County, 1945). Most of these cases held that state labor relations acts or federal labor statutes do not apply to city or state employees.

[90] *City of Springfield* v. *Clause*, 356 Mo. 1239, 206 S.W. 2d 539 (1947).

matter of bargaining and contract." This is so because the questions at issue involve the exercise of legislative powers, and they cannot be delegated away by those to whom the Constitution gives them. It should be added that governmental appropriations are not made out of any profit motive, but in furtherance of over-all fiscal policies, which often involve important political considerations.[91] It follows from all this, and the courts so hold, that a municipality may not enter into an agreement with a union or group of unions under which it commits itself to employ only union labor.[92] This is regarded as a discrimination against non-union labor. However, the courts of Maryland and New York have taken the position that so long as it is done at the request of the worker, a city may deduct union dues from wages,[93] although the Ohio court has ruled against the check-off on the ground that a municipal corporation is not an "employer" and a civil service appointee is not an "employee" within the meaning of the check-off statute.[94]

In a much quoted letter to the National Federation of Federal Employees, dated August 16, 1937, President Franklin D. Roosevelt wrote:

All government employees should realize that the process of collective bargaining, as usually understood, cannot be transplanted into

[91] See *Railway Mail Assoc.* v. *Murphy*, 180 Misc. 868, 44 N.Y.S. 2d 601 (Sup. Ct. Albany Co. 1943): "Much as we all recognize the value and necessity of collective bargaining in industrial and social life, nonetheless, such bargaining is impossible between the Government and its employees, by reason of the very nature of Government itself. . . . Collective bargaining has no place in government service. The employer is the whole people."

[92] The leading case is *Adams* v. *Brenen*, 177 Ill. 194, 52 N.E. 314, 42 L.R.A. 718, 69 Am. St. Rep. 222 (1898). See Note, "Right of Municipality to Enter into Collective Bargaining Agreement on behalf of Civil Service Employees," *New York University Law Quarterly Review*, XVIII (January, 1941), 247-61; Charles S. Rhyne, *Power of Municipalities to Enter into Labor Union Contracts—A Survey of Law and Experience*, National Institute of Municipal Law Officers, Report No. 76, August, 1941.

[93] *Mugford* v. *Mayor and City Council of Baltimore*, 185 Md. 266, 44 A. 2d 745, 162 A.L.R. 1101 (1945), noted, *University of Pennsylvania Law Review*, XCIV (July, 1946), 427 31; *Kirkpatrick* v. *Rcid*, 193 Misc. 702, 85 N.Y.S. 2d 378 (Sup. Ct. N.Y. Co. 1948).

[94] *Hagerman* v. *Dayton*, 147 Ohio St. 313, 71 N.E. 2d 246, 170 A.L.R. 199 (1947).

the public service. It has its distinct and insurmountable limitations when applied to public personnel management. The very nature and purpose of government make it impossible for administrative officials to represent fully or to bind the employer in mutual discussions with government employee organizations. The employer is the whole people, who speak by means of laws enacted by their representatives in Congress. Accordingly, administrative employees and officials alike are governed and guided, and in many instances restricted, by laws which establish policies, procedures, or rules in personnel matters.

This position is amply reflected in the decisions of American courts.[95]

[95] See *United States* v. *United Mine Workers,* 330 U.S. 258 (1947).

CHAPTER IV

THE RIGHT OF ASSOCIATION AND EXPOSURE BY GOVERNMENT

Usually, it is not very difficult for business corporations to secure state charters, since all states seek to encourage business activity. But many states have special laws dealing with the incorporation of non-profit associations which give administrative officials some discretion to refuse charters under certain circumstances. There seem to be two vaguely defined criteria for such refusal, both of dubious constitutionality. There are some holdings to the effect that the association must be in accord with public policy,[1] and also that the association must not conduct activities already adequately performed by existing organizations.[2]

In March, 1961, however, the New York Court of Appeals served notice that it intended to scrutinize more closely the disposition of applications for charters of incorporation.[3] The

[1] See, e.g., *In re Mazzini Cultural Center*, 185 Misc. 1031, 58 N.Y.S. 2d 529 (Sup. Ct. Kings Co. 1945); *In re Patriotic Citizenship Assoc.*, 53 N.Y.S. 2d 595 (Sup. Ct. Kings Co. 1945).

[2] See, e.g., *In re Marine Corps Veterans Foundation*, 79 N.Y.S. 2d 18 (Sup. Ct. Kings Co. 1948); *In re Voters Alliance for Americans of German Ancestry*, 64 N.Y.S. 2d 298 (Sup. Ct. N.Y. Co. 1946); Comment, "State Control over Political Organizations: First Amendment Checks on Powers of Regulation," *Yale Law Journal*, LXVI (February, 1957), 545–66.

[3] *Association for the Preservation of Freedom of Choice, Inc.* v. *Shapiro*, 9 N.Y.2d 376, 174 N.E.2d 487 (1961). On this case see comments in *Howard*

case involved an application for a charter filed by a group having as its purpose the promotion of racial segregation, and having the title, Association for the Preservation of Freedom of Choice. The New York Membership Corporation Law provides that five or more persons may become a membership corporation "for any lawful purpose," with the approval of a Justice of the state supreme court. In this instance the Justice had denied incorporation on the ground of "public policy," his position being that the proposed corporation would be "injurious to the community." The Justice took the view that there was no constitutional or statutory requirement that a "hate group" be given a corporate charter. The Court of Appeals disagreed, holding that the range of judicial power is to determine whether the proposed incorporation is for a lawful purpose, and this was described as a "comparatively simple and narrow judicial function." The Justice, the court ruled, does not have the authority to grant or deny applications based on his personal notions of what is contrary to public policy or injurious to the community. The court declared that "the public policy of the State is not violated by purposes which are not unlawful." Speaking for the court majority, Judge Foster said that "the test as to what may be injurious to the community is too vague, indefinite and elusive to serve as an objective judicial standard. Within such a scope the individual Justice would be at liberty to indulge in his own personal predilections as to the purposes of a proposed corporation, and impose his own personal views as to the social, political and economic matters involved. This is the direct antithesis of judicial objectivity, especially in an *ex parte* proceeding where no evidence is taken." The only test, the court insisted, was whether the purposes are unlawful, and it pointed out that it is perfectly lawful for an individual or a group of individuals to agitate for the change of any law, even for a change in the form of government, provided that there is no advocacy of force or violence. Further, it was pointed out that the approval of a corporate

---

Law Journal, VI (June, 1960), 169–78; *Cornell Law Quarterly*, XLVI (Winter, 1961), 290–305.

charter does not imply approval of the views of its sponsors.[4] Two members of the Court of Appeals dissented, taking the position that the state should not be compelled to lend its prestige to a group whose objectives are a contradiction of existing state law. They thought that a lawful purpose must be in conformity with the spirit as well as the letter of the law, and that it must be in harmony with the explicitly defined public policy of the state, which is strongly opposed to discrimination based on race, color, or creed.

In any event, it is clear that corporations, whether for profit or not, are entitled to the enjoyment of basic constitutional guaranties. While the "liberty" guaranties of the Due Process clauses of the Constitution are construed as applying only to natural persons,[5] corporations are regarded as persons within the meaning of the "property" part of these guaranties,[6] and by extending the meaning of "property" the Supreme Court has protected the "liberty" of corporations,[7] and legal remedies have also been given to the agents of unincorporated associations.[8]

On the other hand, ever since the end of World War II, and as a consequence largely of "cold war" pressures, questions have arisen regarding the right of government to inquire into the facts of membership in certain types of associations. It is now established that it is constitutionally permissible for the state and national governments to ask individuals whether they are or have ever been members of the Communist Party,[9] and

[4] Cf. *Conversion Center Charter Case*, 388 Pa. 239, 10 A. 2d 107 (1957), where the appellate court granted a charter, after denial in the court below, to a group whose purpose was the conversion of Roman Catholics.

[5] See, e.g., *Pierce v. Society of Sisters*, 268 U.S. 510, 535 (1925); *Western Turf Assoc. v. Greenberg*, 204 U.S. 359, 363 (1907); *Northwestern National Life Ins. Co. v. Riggs*, 203 U.S. 243, 255 (1906).

[6] See, e.g., *Liggett Co. v. Baldridge*, 278 U.S. 105 (1928); *Smyth v. Ames*, 169 U.S. 466, 522 (1898).

[7] See, e.g., *Pierce v. Society of Sisters*, 268 U.S. 510, 535 (1925); *Grosjean v. American Press Co.*, 297 U.S. 233, 244 (1936); *Joseph Burstyn, Inc. v. Wilson*, 343 U.S. 495 (1952); *Pennekamp v. Florida*, 328 U.S. 331 (1946).

[8] See, e.g., *Hague v. C.I.O.*, 307 U.S. 496 (1939); *Thomas v. Collins*, 323 U.S. 516 (1945); *Thornhill v. Alabama*, 310 U.S. 88 (1940).

[9] *Barenblatt v. United States*, 360 U.S. 109 (1959); *Barsky v. United States*, 167 F. 2d 241 (D.C. Cir. 1948), *cert. denied*, 334 U.S. 843 (1941);

to determine whether public employees are members of subversive associations.[10] The rights of speech and assembly, the Pennsylvania court recently asserted, "do not extend to freedom to meet with others, knowingly and deliberately, for the discussion of plans to overthrow the government by force or violence," and accordingly it ruled that a nurse in a city hospital could be required to state whether she was, knowingly, a member of an organization advocating overthrow of government by unlawful means.[11] In fact, the federal government now has a considerable body of legislation which requires individuals to disclose certain facts of association about themselves. Thus, the Taft-Hartley Act of 1947 required the officers of trade unions, as a condition of enjoying access to the facilities of the National Labor Relations Board, to sign affidavits of non-Communist membership, and the requirement was upheld by the Supreme Court.[12] The McCarran Internal Security Act of 1950[13] requires registration with the Attorney General of

United States v. Josephson, 165 F. 2d 82 (2d Cir. 1947), cert. denied, 333 U.S. 838 (1948); Lawson v. United States, 176 F. 2d 49 (D.C. Cir. 1949); cert. denied, 339 U.S. 934 (1950); State v. James, 36 Wash. 2d 882, 221 P. 2d 482 (1950).

[10] See Bailey v. Richardson, 182 F. 2d 46 (D.C. Cir. 1950), affirmed by an evenly divided court, 341 U.S. 918 (1951); Garner v. Board of Public Works of Los Angeles, 341 U.S. 716 (1951) (municipal employees); Lerner v. Casey, 357 U.S. 468 (1958) (city subway conductor); Beilan v. Board of Education, 357 U.S. 399 (1958) (school teacher); Thorp v. Board of Trustees of Newark, 6 N.J. 498, 79 A. 2d 462 (1951), judgment vacated for mootness, 342 U.S. 803 (1951) (school teacher); Ex parte Coon, 44 Cal. App. 2d 531, 112 P. 2d 767 (1941) (employee of state relief administration). See Ralph S. Brown, Jr., Loyalty and Security (New Haven: Yale University Press, 1958).

[11] Fitzgerald v. City of Philadelphia, 376 Pa. 379, 386, 102 A. 2d 887, 891, 18 A.L.R. 2d 268 (1954). See Roger C. Cramton, "The Supreme Court and State Power To Deal with Subversion and Loyalty," Minnesota Law Review, XLIII (May, 1959), 1025–82.

[12] American Communications Assoc. v. Douds, 339 U.S. 382 (1950). This requirement was dropped by the Labor-Management Reporting and Disclosure Act of 1959, 73 Stat. 519, 29 U.S.C. § 401 et seq. (1960).

[13] 64 Stat. 987, §§ 7, 8, 50 U.S.C. §§ 781 et seq. See Communist Party v. Subversive Activities Control Board, 351 U.S. 115 (1956); Communist Party v. Subversive Activities Control Board, 361 U.S. 1 (1961). Membership in subversive organizations is made an offense in the Smith Act of

"Communist-action" organizations, together with the names and addresses of all officers and members, and of "Communist-front" organizations, with identification of their officers. This statute was amended by the Communist Control Act of 1954[14] to include "Communist-infiltrated organizations." All foreign agents, whether employed by governments or by organizations subsidized by foreign governments, must register under the Foreign Agents Registration Act of 1938, as amended.[15] The Voorhis Anti-Propaganda Act of 1940[16] provides for the registration with the Attorney General of all organizations under foreign control which participate in civilian military or political activity. Federal laws require many other classes of people to register, including aliens,[17] lobbyists with Congress,[18] and persons who own publications which use second class mailing privileges.[19]

The Supreme Court is willing to permit the states to go a long way in prying into the membership of associations alleged to be subversive. Thus in the recent case of *Uphaus* v. *Wyman*[20] the Court upheld a conviction for civil contempt where a witness testifying before a New Hampshire legislative investigating committee refused to name certain persons whose identity the

---

1940, 54 Stat. 670, § 2 (3). See *Dennis* v. *United States,* 341 U.S. 494 (1951); *Scales* v. *United States,* 367 U.S. 203 (1961).

[14] 68 Stat. 775, 50 U.S.C. §§ 41-4 (1958). For a construction of the California Subversive Organization Registration Act of 1941 see *People* v. *Noble,* 68 Cal. App. 2d 853, 158 P. 2d 225 (1945).

[15] 52 Stat. 631 (1938), as amended, 53 Stat. 1244 (1939), 56 Stat. 248 (1942), 64 Stat. 399 (1950), 22 U.S.C. §§ 601, 611–16 (1958). See *Viereck* v. *United States,* 318 U.S. 236 (1943).

[16] 51 Stat. 1201 (1940), 18 U.S.C. § 2386 (1958).

[17] 66 Stat. 224 (1952), 8 U.S.C. §§ 1302, 1303 (1958). See *Hines* v. *Davidowitz,* 312 U.S. 52 (1941).

[18] 60 Stat. 839 (1946), 2 U.S.C. §§ 261–70 (1958), upheld in *United States* v. *Harriss,* 347 U.S. 612 (1954). See Note, "Registration of Groups Tending To Influence Public Opinion," *Columbia Law Review,* XLVIII (May, 1948), 589–605.

[19] 37 Stat. 553 (1923), 39 U.S.C. § 233 (1958), upheld in *Lewis Publishing Co.* v. *Morgan,* 229 U.S. 288 (1913).

[20] 360 U.S. 72 (1959).

investigation was seeking to establish. Uphaus had been Executive Director of World Fellowship, Inc., a voluntary corporation organized under the laws of New Hampshire which maintained a summer camp in the state. In defiance of a subpoena, Uphaus, who testified as to his own activities, declined to supply the names of all persons who had attended the camp during two previous summers. Dividing five to four, the Supreme Court overruled several objections, including the argument that the state's action violated the rights of free speech and association. Speaking for the Court, Mr. Justice Clark maintained that the public interests involved overbalanced the private interests in associational privacy. The state, he said, is legitimately concerned with the presence of subversives in the state, and the attorney general of New Hampshire, who conducted the investigation, was found to have reason to believe that the guests might have been subversive persons. It was noted, for example, that at least nineteen speakers at the camp had Communist affiliations. Thus it was felt that the state had established the existence of a nexus between the World Fellowship and subversive activities. Since the state regards the Communist Party as posing a serious threat to its security, the Court majority concluded that the investigation had been undertaken in the interest of self-preservation, which is the ultimate value in any society. "This governmental interest," said Mr. Justice Clark, "outweighs individual rights in an associational privacy which, however real in other circumstances, . . . were here tenuous at best." For it was noted that the camp operated as a public one, required by New Hampshire law to maintain a register open to police inspection. It was thus concluded that the disclosure of the names of the guests would be an inescapable incident of an investigation into the presence of subversive persons within the state.[21]

Still more recently, during its 1960–61 Term, the United States Supreme Court rendered several additional decisions

[21] The four dissenting Justices could find no rational connection with a discernible legislative purpose. They thought that what was involved was overwhelmingly "a roving self-contained investigation of individual and group behavior, and behavior in a constitutionally protected area." They insisted that there was no showing that this simple, wide-ranging exposure campaign was designed to implement a valid legislative purpose, but was merely exposure purely for the sake of exposure.

which drew the line in favor of the public interest in disclosure in cases involving membership in the Communist Party. In two important cases it ruled again that the refusal of a witness to tell a congressional committee whether he was a member of the Communist Party was punishable as contempt.[22] In two other cases the Court held that a state has not denied due process where, because of refusal to answer questions concerning membership in the Communist Party, it denies admission to the bar.[23] The Court felt that the public interest in determining the fitness of men to practice law outweighed the interest in associational freedom. Indeed, since bar committee interrogations are conducted in private, it could see "no likelihood that deterrence of association may result from foreseeable private action."[24] In still another case the Court finally upheld an order of the Subversive Activities Control Board.[25] Speaking for the Court, Mr. Justice Frankfurter ruled that "rational interests high in the scale of national concern"[26] justified the regulation through registration of an association found by Congress to be a foreign-directed conspiracy against the safety of constitutional government.

Most significant of all the cases decided in the spring of 1961 was *Scales* v. *United States*,[27] in which the Court upheld, by a five to four vote, the constitutionality of the clause of the

[22] *Wilkinson* v. *United States*, 365 U.S. 399 (1961); *Braden* v. *United States*, 365 U.S. 431 (1961). The vote in both of these cases was five to four.

[23] *Konigsberg* v. *State Bar of California*, 366 U.S. 36 (1961); *In re Anastaplo*, 366 U.S. 82 (1961). The Court was divided five to four in both cases. In *Cohen* v. *Hurley*, 366 U.S. 117 (1961), the Court sustained the disbarment of an attorney who refused on self-incrimination grounds to answer questions in an investigation of professional misconduct taking the form of "ambulance-chasing." In *Lathrop* v. *Donohue*, 367 U.S. 820 (1961), the Court ruled that a state may constitutionally require all lawyers to belong to an integrated bar association.

[24] 366 U.S. at 52.

[25] *Communist Party of the U.S.* v. *Subversive Activities Control Board*, 367 U.S. 1 (1961).

[26] *Ibid.* at 73.

[27] 367 U.S. 203. In *Noto* v. *United States*, 367 U.S. 290 (1961), the Court set aside a conviction of violating the membership clause of the Smith Act because of insufficiency of evidence.

Smith Act which makes it a felony to acquire or hold knowing membership in any organization which advocates the overthrow of government by force or violence. Scales was convicted of belonging to the Communist Party when he knew of its illegal purpose. The Court emphasized that the trial judge had properly construed the statute as requiring proof that the Communist Party advocated action to overthrow the government violently, and that the defendant must be shown to have been an active member who knew about the Party's illegal advocacy and intent to bring about violent overthrow as soon as circumstances would permit. A combination promoting criminal activity is not the sort of association, the Court ruled, which is protected by the First Amendment. "Any thought," said Mr. Justice Harlan, "that due process puts beyond the reach of the criminal law all individual associational relationships, unless accompanied by the commission of specific acts of criminality, is dispelled by familiar concepts of the law of conspiracy and complicity." Since it is clear, he argued, that society has the power to punish dangerous behavior, it cannot be powerless to deal with those who work to bring about that behavior. There is no reason, he declared, why one who actively and knowingly works in the ranks of an organization which engages in criminal activity, with the intention of contributing to the success of specifically illegal purposes and activities, should be immune from prosecution. Finally, Mr. Justice Harlan noted that the membership clause of the Smith Act, as construed, did not cut deeper into the freedom of association than was necessary to deal with substantive evils that Congress has a right to prevent.

The four dissenting members of the Court disagreed on grounds of statutory construction, but Justices Black and Douglas went much farther to argue that the decision was a serious blow to the freedoms guaranteed by the First Amendment. Said Mr. Justice Douglas: "We legalize today guilt by association, sending a man to prison when he committed no unlawful act. Today's break with tradition is a serious one. It borrows from the totalitarian philosophy." He stressed the fact that Scales had not been charged with the commission of a single illegal act; the crime is belief, and while the belief in question was unpopular and to most people revolting, nevertheless he thought it was not permissible to punish beliefs in the light of the Bill of Rights.

On the other hand, the Court has defended important rights of associational membership where the association is not subversive and is not engaged in other unlawful activities. Here the interest in privacy and the right to associate take priority over asserted public interests. This point has been driven home in recent years in the campaign of some southern states against the National Association for the Advancement of Colored People, which has been the spearhead of the drive of the Negroes of the country for the enjoyment of equal rights. Far from being subversive, the overriding purpose of the NAACP is to translate into actuality, for all people regardless of race or color, basic constitutional rights. Those who seek to deny their rights are subversive. American Negroes have not been seduced by Communism,[28] and Mr. J. Edgar Hoover, the esteemed Director of the Federal Bureau of Investigation, recently pointed out that NAACP has always vigorously denounced and fought Communist attempts at infiltration.[29]

Since the school segregation cases of 1954[30] there has been a sustained and varied legislative and administrative harassment of NAACP in many southern states.[31] The attack has proceeded on many fronts. Since one of the principal functions of NAACP is to manage and finance law suits in behalf of individual Negro complainants,[32] southern states have adopted new and more stringent laws dealing with the offenses of champerty,

[28] See Wilson Record, *The Negro and the Communist Party* (Chapel Hill: University of North Carolina Press, 1951).

[29] *Masters of Deceit* (New York: Holt, 1958), pp. 246–47, 252.

[30] *Brown* v. *Board of Education*, 347 U.S. 483 (1954).

[31] See Walter F. Murphy, "The South Counterattacks: The Anti-NAACP Laws," *Western Political Quarterly*, XII (June, 1959), 371–90; Robert B. McKay, "The Repression of Civil Rights as an Aftermath of the School Segregation Cases," *Howard Law Journal*, IV (January, 1958), 9–35; "Freedom of Association," *Race Relations Law Reporter*, IV (Spring, 1959), 207–36; Comment, "Group Action, Civil Rights and Freedom of Association," *Northwestern University Law Review*, LV (July–August, 1959), 390–404.

[32] See Clement E. Vose, "NAACP Strategy in the Covenant Cases," *Western Reserve Law Review*, VI (Winter, 1955), 101–45.

maintenance, and barratry—which, generally speaking, are aimed at "stirring up litigation"[33]—or have intensified the enforcement of existing laws of this type.[34] In addition, these states have expanded the enforcement of the criminal law, especially as regards breach of the peace and disorderly conduct, denied public employment to members of NAACP, and embarked upon fresh regulation of the local aspects of foreign corporations under general corporation laws. The principal weapon has been to seek to identify publicly the names of the members of the various NAACP chapters, thus exposing them to severe community reprisals, such as the loss of employment, the calling or denial of bank loans, foreclosure of mortgages, and assorted types of violence.

The effort to disclose the identity of the members of NAACP has taken many forms: exploitation of the traditional power of state legislatures to conduct investigations,[35] enactment of new registration statutes requiring submission of the names of contributors and members,[36] and other stratagems

[33] Max Radin, "Maintenance by Champerty," *California Law Review,* XXIV (November, 1935), 48–78. See *Gammons* v. *Johnson,* 76 Minn. 76, 81, 78 N.W. 1035, 1037 (1899): "The general purposes of the law against champerty and maintenance and barratry was to prevent officious intermeddlers from stirring up strife and contention by vexatious or speculative litigation, which would disturb the peace of society, lead to corrupt practices, and prevent the remedial process of the law."

[34] See "Inciting Litigation," *Race Relations Law Reporter,* III (December, 1958), 1257–77.

[35] See *Gibson* v. *Florida Legislative Investigation Com.,* 108 So. 2d 729 (Fla. 1958), *cert. denied,* 360 U.S. 919 (1959). While this case upheld a wide legislative power to investigate on this score, it involved only an investigation of communism, and the court cautioned that it should not be used to conduct witch-hunts, or "merely for the sake of disclosure." For recent legislation authorizing investigations see S.C. Acts 1956, Act 920; La. H. Con. Res. No. 27, 1954, and No. 9, 1956; Va. Laws, 1956, Extra Sess., cc. 34, 37; Ga. Res. Act 18, 1958; Ga. House Res. Nos. 8, 11, 1957; Fla. Laws 1956, c. 31498; Fla. Laws 1957, c. 57–125; Miss. H.B. 1956, c. 880, Miss. S.B. 1958, c. 1973 (State Sovereignty Commission); Ark. Acts 1957, No. 83; Ark. Acts 1958, No. 13 (State Sovereignty Commission).

[36] See Ark. Acts 1957, No. 85; Ark. Acts 1958, Nos. 10, 12 (Extraordinary Sess.); Ark. Acts 1959, No. 225; S.C. Acts 1957, No. 223; Tenn. Code Ann. § 39–5001-7 (Supp. 1958); Tenn. Code Ann. § 39–827-34 (Supp. 1958); Tex. H.B. 1957, No. 239 (not enacted following opinion of Attorney

designed to bring into the open the names of members of the Association.[37]

The Supreme Court disposed of two major cases involving this issue of disclosure of membership lists in 1958 and 1960, and in both cases the Justices were unanimously on the side of the NAACP membership.[38] In the first case, *NAACP* v. *Alabama*,[39] the Court had before it a judgment of civil contempt against the Association which Alabama courts had entered when the Association refused to comply with a court order requiring the production of its membership lists. The issue arose when the state's attorney general brought an equity suit, under the Alabama foreign corporations act, with which NAACP had never complied in the belief that it was exempt, to enjoin further activity of NAACP, a non-profit New York corporation, in the state. The court granted an immediate restraining order, and the state then moved for the production of many records and papers, including the names of all agents and members. When the Association refused to comply with the production order so far as the membership lists were concerned, it was held in civil contempt and fined $100,000.

General of Texas, May 21, 1957); Va. Code, §§ 18-349.9–.17 (Supp. 1959); Ga. Acts 1958, No. 321; Louisiana Rev. Stat., tit. 12, §§ 401 *et seq.* (1950).

[37] Joseph B. Robison, "Protection of Associations from Compulsory Disclosure of Membership," *Columbia Law Review,* LVIII (May, 1958), 614–49; Note, "The Constitutional Right of Anonymity: Free Speech, Disclosure and the Devil," *Yale Law Journal,* LXX (June, 1961), 1084–1128.

[38] One case reached the Court testing the validity of the new Virginia laws on registration and barratry, which were designed to discourage litigation on school integration, *Harrison* v. *NAACP,* 360 U.S. 167 (1959), but it was held that the federal district court should have abstained from deciding the merits of the issues until the state courts had a reasonable opportunity to construe the statutes. Three Justices, dissenting, protested that where there has been state defiance of the citizen's constitutional rights, the customary reasons for showing this sort of deference to state institutions vanish.

[39] 357 U.S. 449 (1958). See notes in *Howard Law Journal,* V (January, 1959), 112–15; *Ohio State Law Journal,* XX (Winter, 1959), 123–26; *George Washington Law Review,* XXVII (June, 1959), 653–72; *Cleveland-Marshall Law Review,* X (January, 1961), 104–22.

All the Justices of the Supreme Court agreed that the state judgment must be reversed on the ground that the production order violated due process. They took the position that group association undeniably enhances effective advocacy of both public and private points of view, and that there is therefore a "close nexus" between the freedoms of speech and assembly. "It is beyond debate," said Mr. Justice Harlan, "that freedom to engage in association for the advancement of beliefs and ideas is an inseparable aspect of the 'liberty' assured by the Due Process Clause of the Fourteenth Amendment." It is important to note that this was the first time that the Supreme Court ever used the phrase, "the right of association," in a forthright constitutional holding. Mr. Justice Harlan added that "Of course, it is immaterial whether the beliefs sought to be advanced by association pertain to political, economic, religious or cultural matters, and state action which may have the effect of curtailing the freedom to associate is subject to the closest scrutiny."[40] The Court held, further, that it was not a decisive fact that Alabama had taken no direct action to restrict the right of NAACP members to associate freely, since it must recognize that in the area of indispensable liberties abridgement may follow from various forms of governmental action. "It it hardly a novel perception," said Mr. Justice Harlan, "that compelled disclosure of affiliation with groups engaged in advocacy may constitute as effective a restraint on freedom of association," as other forms of action previously held to be interferences with freedom of speech. "This Court has recognized," he noted, "the vital relationship between freedom to associate and privacy in one's associations. . . . Inviolability of privacy in group association may in many circumstances be indispensable to preservation of freedom of association, particularly where a group espouses dissident beliefs."[41] Thus the Court concluded that the production order entailed the likelihood of a substantial restraint upon the exercise by members of NAACP of their right to freedom of association. It was noted that NAACP had shown incontrovertibly that on past occasions revelation of identity of rank-and-file members had exposed them to economic reprisal, loss of employment, threats of physical coer-

[40] 357 U.S. at 460.　　　　　[41] *Id.* at 462.

cion, and other manifestations of public hostility. It follows that compelled disclosure of membership is likely to affect adversely the ability of NAACP and its members to pursue their collective effort to foster beliefs which they have an admitted right to advocate. And the Court declared that it was not a sufficient answer to say that whatever repression may come would be due to private community pressures, and not to state action, since the crucial fact was that an exertion of state power would have invoked the pressure.

The Court took the position that Alabama had not demonstrated an interest in obtaining the disclosures it was after, sufficient to justify their deterrent effect on the free exercise of the constitutionally protected right of association. Alabama declared that its interest was to determine whether NAACP was conducting an intrastate business in violation of its foreign corporation registration statute. The Court ruled that the disclosure of the names of the members of NAACP had no substantial bearing on this issue. Finally the Court distinguished its 1928 decision in the Zimmerman case[42] on the ground that it was based on the nature of the Klan, which engaged in acts of unlawful intimidation and violence, and which made no effort to comply with any provisions of the New York statute and declined to give the state any information at all. In contrast, it was pointed out that NAACP had not refused to comply with Alabama law, but only declined to give the names of its members. It had even been willing to give the names of its officers.

The issue of compulsory disclosure of NAACP membership lists reached the Supreme Court again in 1960, in *Bates* v. *City of Little Rock*,[43] and again by unanimous vote the position taken in the Alabama case was reaffirmed. Whereas in the earlier case the local effort was tied to a purported attempt to enforce the foreign corporation law, in the case of Little Rock an attempt was made to tie it to the local taxing power. Pursuant to statute, Little Rock had for some years, by ordinance, imposed annual license taxes on a broad variety of businesses, occupations, and professions. An amendment adopted in 1957 required any organization operating within the city to give the

[42] *New York ex rel. Bryant* v. *Zimmerman,* 278 U.S. 63 (1928).

[43] 361 U.S. 516.

City Clerk, on request, certain information, including the names of all who paid dues, assessments, or contributions, and provided that all such information shall be public. The custodian of the local branch of NAACP supplied all the information demanded by the ordinance except the names of members and contributors, on the stated grounds of fear of harassment, economic reprisals, bodily harm, and violation of the Constitution. Evidence at the trial showed that many members declined to renew their memberships because of the ordinance.

Reversing the conviction in the state courts, the Supreme Court pointed out that the framers of the Constitution regarded the right of peaceable assembly, like freedom of speech and press, "to lie at the foundation of a government based upon the consent of an informed citizenry . . . ," and that "it is now beyond dispute that freedom of association for the purpose of advancing ideas and airing grievances is protected by the Due Process Clause of the Fourteenth Amendment from invasion by the States." Furthermore, this freedom is protected "not only against heavy-handed frontal attack, but also from being stifled by more subtle governmental interference."[44] The Court was satisfied that the record showed that the compulsory disclosure of membership lists in this instance "would work a significant interference with the freedom of association of their members," since there was substantial incontroverted evidence that public identification of memberships would be followed by harassment, threats of bodily harm, fear of community hostility, and economic reprisals, and that former members had been induced to withdraw and potential ones not to join. The Court concluded, therefore, that the threat of "substantial government encroachment upon important and traditional aspects of individual freedom is neither speculative nor remote."[45]

To be sure, the city of Little Rock asserted its interest in the taxing power, which is conceded by all to be a basic function of government, but the Court could find "no relevant correlation" between the city's power to impose occupation license

[44] *Ibid.* at 522–23. Cf. *Talley* v. *California,* 362 U.S. 60 (1960), which held unconstitutional a city ordinance which forbade public distributions of handbills which did not bear on their face the name and address of the author, publisher, and distributor.

[45] *Ibid.* at 524.

taxes and the compulsory disclosure and publication of membership lists. For the city had never asserted a tax claim against NAACP, and the Association had never claimed an exemption. Thus the city had failed to show "a controlling justification for the deterrence of free association."

In December, 1960, the Supreme Court once again came to the defense of associational freedom in *Shelton* v. *Tucker*,[46] though by the close margin of a five to four vote. The Court held unconstitutional an Arkansas statute adopted in 1958 which provided that, as a condition of employment in any state-supported school or college, every teacher must file annually an affidavit listing without limitation every organization to which he has belonged or regularly contributed money within the preceding five years. The Court majority agreed with the minority that there is no doubt about the right of a state to investigate the competence and fitness of those it hires to teach in its schools, and that there is no constitutional requirement that a teacher's classroom conduct should be the sole basis of determining fitness.[47] On the other hand, the majority thought it indisputable that "to compel a teacher to disclose his every associational tie is to impair the teacher's right of free association, a right closely allied to freedom of speech and a right which, like free speech, lies at the foundation of a free society."[48] Furthermore, said Mr. Justice Stewart, this interference with personal freedom "is conspicuously accented when the teacher serves at the absolute will of those to whom the disclosure must be made. . . ." As a matter of fact, he observed that even without disclosure, the pressure on a teacher to avoid any ties which might displease those who control his professional destiny would be constant and heavy. The issue was not whether Arkansas can ask its teachers about certain specified associational ties which are relevant to the issue of their professional fitness, but whether it may ask every teacher to disclose every single organization with which he has been associated over a five-year period. Since the scope of the inquiry is completely unlimited, it applies to all sorts of mem-

[46] 364 U.S. 479.

[47] See *Beilan* v. *Board of Education of Philadelphia*, 357 U.S. 399 (1958).

[48] 364 U.S. at 485–86.

berships—religious, political, professional, avocational, etc.—many of which have no possible bearing upon the teacher's fitness. Thus the Court concluded that "the statute's comprehensive interference with associational freedom goes far beyond what might be justified in the exercise of the State's legitimate inquiry into the fitness and competency of its teachers."[49]

The dissenting Justices argued that the statute was valid on its face, since they saw a rational relation between the required disclosure and a governmental interest justifying it. But they agreed that if it turns out that the information is used to further a scheme of terminating the employment of teachers solely because of their membership in unpopular organizations, such use would violate due process. A record of discriminatory administration would make a difference, but the case went up without a record of administration. It follows that while the Justices were divided five to four in ruling on the statute on its face, they shared a very wide area of agreement.

Finally, in May, 1961, the Supreme Court held two Louisiana statutes unconstitutional which, as applied to NAACP, required the state chapter to file a list of the names and addresses of all its officers and members, and also affidavits testifying to the fact that none of the officers of any group with which it was affiliated was subversive.[50] It is now well established, said Mr. Justice Douglas, that where "disclosure of membership lists results in reprisals against and hostility to the members, disclosure is not required." In this area, he added, "any regulation must be highly selective in order to survive challenge under the First Amendment."[51] And he closed with the observation that "regulatory measures . . . no matter how sophisticated, cannot be employed in purpose or in effect to stifle, penalize, or curb the exercise of First Amendment rights."[52]

[49] 364 U.S. at 490.

[50] *Louisiana ex rel. Gremillion* v. *NAACP*, 366 U.S. 293 (1961).

[51] *Ibid.* at 296.   [52] *Ibid.* at 297.

CHAPTER V

THE BAD ASSOCIATION
AND BAD ASSOCIATES

THE ANTI-KLAN LAWS

The revival of the Ku Klux Klan, particularly in the South, in the years immediately following World War I,[1] quickly led to a situation which tested the limits of the right of association. For a number of reasons the Klan was a serious problem: it operated in secret; it functioned through a membership bound by oaths; it regularly resorted to the use of masks to conceal identity; and above all, it depended upon stirring up fear and prejudice through intimidation and the disregard of law. In short, terrorism was one of its standard weapons, and under the cloak of its operations, murders, lynchings, the bombing of homes, arsons, and whippings of victims occurred. As a result, some state legislatures began to adopt anti-Klan laws.[2]

The earliest of these laws, and the best known, was that of the state of New York, adopted in 1923.[3] Known as the Walker

[1] See John M. Mecklin, *The Ku Klux Klan* (New York: Harcourt, Brace, 1924); Stanley Frost, *The Challenge of the Klan* (Indianapolis: Bobbs-Merrill, 1924); Gustavus Myers, *History of Bigotry in the United States* (New York: Random House, 1943), chaps. xiv–xvi.

[2] See Jack Swertfeger, Jr., "Anti-Mask and Anti-Klan Laws," *Journal of Public Law*, I (Spring, 1952), 182–97.

[3] N.Y. Sess. Laws 1923, c. 664. The statute was amended with N.Y. Sess. Laws 1925, c. 251, and is now § 53 of the N.Y. Civil Rights Law. Louisiana adopted an anti-Klan law in 1924, La. Acts 1924, No. 2, now La. Rev. Stat. §§ 12: 401–9 (1950). The Louisiana Law is much broader than that of New York, applying to all "fraternal, patriotic, charitable,

Law, it provides—for it is still on the books—that with the exception of labor unions, student fraternities and sororities, and benevolent orders, all oath-bound organizations having more than twenty members must submit annual registration statements, including a list of officers and roster of membership, to the secretary of state. The statute was aimed at the Klan, and when a Klan officer named George W. Bryant refused to file the necessary registration statement, he was arrested for violating the law. Bryant sued for habeas corpus in the state courts on the ground that the law was unconstitutional. The New York Supreme Court dismissed the petition,[4] the Appellate Division affirmed by a four to one vote,[5] and the New York Court of Appeals affirmed unanimously, Judge Pound declaring that "the Legislature may take notice of the potentialities of evil in secret societies, and may regulate them reasonably. . . ."[6]

In *New York ex rel. Bryant* v. *Zimmerman*,[7] decided in 1928, the Supreme Court sustained the constitutionality of the statute.[8] Speaking for the Court, Mr. Justice Van Devanter declared that the liberty of association, "like most other personal rights, must yield to the rightful exertion of the police power.

---

benevolent, literary, scientific, athletic, military, or social" organizations, exempting only "regularly organized churches or National Guard organizations." While this law was not used effectively against the Klan, it has been revived recently for action against the NAACP.

4 *People ex rel. Bryant* v. *Sheriff of Erie County*, 123 Misc. 859, 206 N.Y.S. 533 (Sup. Ct. Erie Co. 1924). The Court said: "It is a matter of common knowledge that this organization functions largely at night, its members disguised by hoods and gowns, and doing things calculated to strike terror into the minds of the people."

5 *People ex rel. Bryant* v. *Zimmerman*, 213 App. Div. 414, 210 N.Y.S. 269 (4th Dept. 1925). The Court concluded that the statute was a valid "police regulation for the general welfare and safety of the people of the state."

6 *People ex rel. Bryant* v. *Zimmerman*, 241 N.Y. 405, 410, 150 N.E. 497, 498 (1926).

7 278 U.S. 63.

8 All the Justices agreed on the merits, but Mr. Justice McReynolds voted to dismiss the writ of error on the technical procedural grounds that Bryant had not properly raised the federal question, and that the real controversy between the parties involved no substantial federal question.

There can be no doubt that under that power the State may prescribe and apply to associations having an oath-bound membership any reasonable regulation calculated to confine their purposes and activities within limits which are consistent with the rights of others and the public welfare."[9] He thought that the registration requirement was reasonable,

. . . on the two-fold theory that the State within whose territory and under whose protection the association exists is entitled to be informed of its nature and purpose, of whom it is composed and by whom its activities are conducted, and that requiring this information to be supplied for the public files will operate as an effective or substantial deterrent from the violation of public and private right to which the association might be tempted if such a disclosure were not required. The requirement is not arbitrary or oppressive, but reasonable and likely to be of real effect.[10]

Finally the Court rejected "the main contention" advanced by Bryant, that by making the exceptions it did, the statute violated the equal protection clause. It was concluded that the legislative classification was reasonable and not arbitrary because the Court felt that the legislature could reasonably conclude that for the Klan (and associations like it), there was a "manifest tendency . . . to make the secrecy surrounding its purposes and membership a cloak for acts and conduct inimical to personal rights and public welfare. . . ."[11]

The Court referred to extensive testimony regarding the Klan, particularly to a recent congressional hearing,[12] and noted that the legislature had before it incontroverted evidence

. . . that the order was a revival of the Ku Klux Klan of an earlier time with additional features borrowed from the Know-Nothing and the American Protective Association orders of other periods; that its membership was limited to native born, gentile, protestant whites; that in part of its constitution and printed creed it proclaimed the widest freedom for all and full adherence to the Constitution of the United States, in another exacted of its members an oath to shield and preserve "white supremacy," and in still another declared any person actively opposing its principles to be "a dangerous ingredient in the body politic of our country and an enemy

[9] 278 U.S. at 72.   [10] *Ibid.*   [11] *Ibid.*, p. 75.

[12] *Hearings before the Committee on Rules*, House of Representatives, 67th Cong., 1st Sess., 1921, on "The Ku Klux Klan."

to the weal of our national commonwealth"; that it was conducting a crusade against Catholics, Jews and Negroes and stimulating hurtful religious and race prejudices; that it was striving for political power and assuming a sort of guardianship over the administration of local, state and national affairs; and that at times it was taking into its own hands the punishment of what some of its members conceived to be crimes.[13]

It follows from all this, Mr. Justice Van Devanter concluded, that the state courts were right in holding that there was "a real and substantial basis" for the distinction which the statute made between the regulated and the unregulated associations.[14] But it is also worth noting that the Court did not discuss the argument that exposure is repressive and that this was the purpose of the statute.

When, in 1958, the Court had before it a case involving an attack upon the NAACP,[15] it pointed out that the Klan was different. The Court said that "the decision was based on the particular character of the Klan's activities, involving acts of unlawful intimidation and violence, which the Court assumed was before the state legislature when it enacted the statute, and of which the Court took judicial notice."[16] It was also noted that unlike NAACP, the Klan in New York had made no effort at all to comply with any requirements of the state law.

There was a revival of Klan activity, again largely in the South, following World War II, and again the state legislatures began to write new anti-Klan statutes, of which a 1951 South Carolina act is a good sample.[17] Following the example of about

[13] 278 U.S. at 76–77.

[14] The New York courts have ruled that an organization which exacts only a pledge from its members is not within the coverage of this statute, *People* v. *Mueller*, 255 Misc. 316, 7 N.Y.S. 2d 522 (2d Dept. 1938), *appeal dismissed*, 280 N.Y. 669, 20 N.E. 2d 1021 (1939).

[15] *NAACP* v. *Alabama*, 357 U.S. 449 (1958).

[16] *Ibid.* at 465–66.

[17] S.C. Acts 1951, No. 99, p. 132, S.C. Code, § 16-114-17 (1952). See also Ala. Code Ann. tit. 14, § 358 (1) (Supp. 1953); Fla. Gen. Acts 1951, No. 63, p. 115, Fla. Stat. c. 876.11–.21 (1957); Ga. Code Ann. tit. 26, §§ 5301a–11a (1953). See Elizabeth Geyer, "The 'New' Ku Klux Klan," *The Crisis*, LXIII (March, 1956), 139–48.

a dozen other states,[18] this statute prohibits the wearing of masks in public places, and forbids entering upon the premises of another while wearing a mask, without the permission of the owner of the property. The statute also forbids cross-burning in any public place or on any person's property without his prior permission. Several states now have provisions regarding the burning of crosses which are similar to the South Carolina act. States with a "strong" anti-mask law make it a crime to wear a mask in public; the "weak" laws on the subject require proof of intent to commit a breach of the peace. Thus the Tennessee statute forbids people to prowl or ride or walk about masked or in disguise "to the disturbance of the peace, or to the alarming of the citizens. . . ."[19]

The Supreme Court of Wisconsin ruled, in 1925, that a K.K.K. parade on the city streets conducted in an orderly and peaceful manner was not an unlawful assembly, on the theory that experience in the state did not indicate that resentment against the Klan would lead to acts of violence or a tumultuous breach of the peace.[20] On the other hand, the Alabama court ruled in 1949 that when a grand jury is investigating such unlawful acts as terrorism and flogging, it has a lawful right to require an officer of the Federated Ku Klux Klan, an Alabama corporation, to produce certain records in his custody and the membership roster.[21] Refusal to obey a subpoena *duces tecum* was held properly punishable as contempt. The court ruled that the identity of the membership of a private fraternal corporation was not privileged. The court rejected the argu-

[18] See Walter Gellhorn, ed., *The States and Subversion* (Ithaca: Cornell University Press, 1952), p. 403. See, e.g., Calif. Gen. Laws 1947, Act 4707, §1.

[19] Tenn. Code Ann., § 39–2801 (1955). An anti-mask city ordinance was upheld over constitutional objections in *City of Pineville* v. *Marshall,* 222 Ky. 4,299 S.W. 1072 (1927): "Clearly a disguise is a shield and protection to the criminal. . . ."

[20] *Shields* v. *State,* 187 Wis. 448, 204 N.W. 486, 40 A.L.R. 945 (1925). One Justice dissented, arguing that "it is a matter of common knowledge that the Ku Klux Klan is an organization having for its creed certain religious and racial antipathies which have led to disorders, riots, and bloodshed." 187 Wis. at 457, 204 N.W. at 489.

[21] *Ex parte Morris,* 252 Ala. 551, 42 So. 2d 17 (1949).

74

ment that the grand jury was engaged in a mere fishing expedition, pointing out that "one of the major functions of a grand jury is to embark upon inquisitorial expeditions to ferret out crime." The central point of this decision was, of course, that the grand jury was looking into criminal activities, which is the original and classic purpose of the grand jury.

There has been a federal statute on the books directed against Klan activities ever since Congress adopted the Ku Klux Klan Act, or the Antilynching Act, in April, 1871.[22] The key paragraph, which in its present form is Section 241 of the federal criminal code (Title 18) reads as follows:

If two or more persons conspire to injure, oppress, threaten, or intimidate any citizen in the free exercise or enjoyment of any right or privilege secured to him by the Constitution or laws of the United States, or because of his having so exercised the same; or

If two or more persons go in disguise on the highway, or on the premises of another, with intent to prevent or hinder his free exercise or enjoyment of any right or privilege so secured—

They shall be fined not more than $5,000 or imprisoned not more than ten years, or both.

While this statute has never been held invalid, the Supreme Court, from the very beginning, took a narrow view of the rights which fall within its scope. Thus, in 1876, in the landmark case of *United States* v. *Cruikshank*,[23] the Supreme Court ruled that the right of assembly was not a federal right within the meaning of the statute, unless the assembly was called for the purpose of discussing a federal statute or other federal problem. The Court has consistently taken the view that the statute does not embrace the rights set out in the first ten Amendments of the U.S. Constitution, since they apply only to the national government, nor any rights falling within the Fourteenth and Fifteenth Amendments, since they apply only to governments and their agencies or officials. The statute does include such rights as the right to be free from involuntary

[22] Act of April 20, 1871, 17 Stat. 13.

[23] 92 U.S. 542. See Homer Cummings and Carl McFarland, *Federal Justice* (New York: Macmillan, 1937), chaps. xii, xxiv.

servitude,[24] the right to participate in a federal election,[25] the right to inform federal officers of the violation of national laws,[26] and the right to be free from mob violence while in federal custody.[27] While it cannot be said that this statute has no life in it at all, it is still true that it does not have much life.[28]

There are a few other federal statutes which have some bearing upon Klan activities. There have been some prosecutions of Klansmen under the Federal Kidnaping Act (the Lindbergh Law).[29] Other available federal statutes forbid the intimidation of voters in federal elections,[30] and the intimidation of witnesses in federal judicial and administrative proceedings.[31] In some situations the injunctive powers of the federal courts are also available where violence or intimidation infringes upon the operations of federal justice.[32] Furthermore, the National Firearms Act of 1934 forbids the transportation of unregistered firearms in interstate commerce.[33] In this connection it should be pointed out that many states have statutes which prohibit

[24] *Smith* v. *United States,* 157 Fed. 721 (8th Cir. 1907), *cert. denied,* 208 U.S. 618 (1908).

[25] *Ex parte Yarbrough,* 110 U.S. 651 (1884); *United States* v. *Mosley,* 238 U.S. 383 (1915).

[26] *Motes* v. *United States,* 178 U.S. 458 (1900).

[27] *Logan* v. *United States,* 144 U.S. 263 (1892).

[28] See Eugene Gressman, "The Unhappy History of Civil Rights Legislation," *Michigan Law Review,* L (June, 1952), 1323–58; Osmond K. Fraenkel, "The Federal Civil Rights Laws," *Minnesota Law Review,* XXXI (March, 1947), 301–27; Robert K. Carr, *Federal Protection of Civil Rights* (Ithaca: Cornell University Press, 1947).

[29] 18 U.S.C. § 1201. See *Brooks* v. *United States,* 199 F. 2d 336 (4th Cir. 1952); *New York Times,* February 17 and 28, 1952, May 14, 1952, November 17, 1953.

[30] 18 U.S.C. § 594 (the Hatch Act).

[31] 18 U.S.C. §§ 1503, 1505. See Note, "Federal Power To Prosecute Violence against Minority Groups," *Yale Law Journal,* LVII (March, 1948), 855–73.

[32] See *Brewer* v. *Hoxie School District,* 238 F. 2d 91 (8th Cir. 1956).

[33] Act of June 26, 1934, 48 Stat. 1236, 26 U.S.C. § 5855. See *United States* v. *Adams,* 11 F. Supp. 216 (S.D. Fla. 1935).

unauthorized bodies of men from associating themselves together "as a military company with arms."[34]

Finally, it is to be noted that the Ku Klux Klan has been investigated a number of times by the House Committee on Un-American Activities,[35] and that the attorney general has put it on the federal government's list of subversive organizations.[36]

ASSOCIATION WITH BAD PEOPLE

Is it permissible, in a constitutional system committed to the basic principles of personal liberty, for government to punish a man because of the company he keeps? Does the normal right of the individual to associate with whomever he chooses ever have to yield to some overriding social interest spelled out in the law? Such questions as these have often been debated in American legislative bodies and appellate courts.

Whether the state may make keeping "bad" company a crime or an essential element of a crime has usually arisen in situations involving prosecutions for vagrancy. Every state but

[34] Wash. Rev. Stat. Ann. (Remington, 1932), § 2546. For cases upholding the validity of such statutes see *Presser* v. *Illinois*, 116 U.S. 252 (1886); *Com.* v. *Murphy*, 166 Mass. 171, 44 N.E. 138 (1896): "This is a matter affecting the public security, quiet, and good order. . . ." New York and New Jersey enacted statutes, shortly before World War II, aimed at the German-American Bund, which prohibited the public appearance of uniformed private armies. N.Y. Laws, 1939, c. 548; N.J. Laws, 1939, c. 210. Congress has forbidden the unauthorized wearing of the official uniforms of the United States armed forces, Act of June 3, 1916, 39 Stat. 216, 10 U.S.C. § 771. See *Gaston* v. *United States,* 79 App. D.C. 37, 143 F. 2d 10 (1944), *cert. denied*, 322 U.S. 764 (1944). Some states go so far as to forbid the unauthorized use of the uniforms of certain private lawful societies, e.g., Ind. Stat. Ann. (Burns, 1956), § 10-504, construed and sustained in *Hammer* v. *State*, 173 Ind. 199, 89 N.E. 850, 24 L.R.A. (N.S.) 795, 140 Am. St. 248 (1909).

[35] See House Committee on Un-American Activities, *Guide to Subversive Organizations and Publications*, January 2, 1957, p. 151. See also "The Ku Klux Klan," Hearings before the Committee on Rules, House of Representatives, 67th Cong., 1st Sess., 1921; "Senatorial Campaign Expenditures," Hearings before a Special Committee Investigating Expenditures in Senatorial Primary and General Elections, Senate, 69th Cong., 1st Sess., 1926, especially Part 3, pp. 2032 *et seq.* See also House Committee on Un-American Activities, *Preliminary Report on Neo-Fascist and Hate Groups*, December 17, 1954.

[36] 5 Code Fed. Reg. § 210 (App. A, 1949).

West Virginia has some sort of general vagrancy act, and the courts, as a rule, uphold the constitutionality of these statutes as a valid exercise of the police power. "Society recognizes," the Supreme Court of Washington once declared, "that vagrancy is a parasitic disease which, if allowed to spread, will sap the life of that upon which it feeds."[37] Nevertheless, it has been pointed out that these statutes "almost always offend traditional standards of criminal procedure."[38] Since one who is arrested as a vagrant must then prove that he does not fall within the statute, the defendant is generally burdened with a presumption of criminality, contrary to the normal presumption of innocence which an accused person carries with him. Furthermore, the vagrancy laws are so broadly and loosely phrased that the police and the magistrates are at liberty simply to apply their own moral standards according to personal taste. These laws also tend to become instruments of police harassment, and are used for making arrests on mere suspicion, although such arrests are universally regarded as illegal in American jurisdictions.

In spelling out the various ingredients of vagrancy, a considerable number of states have provided in their statutes that it is a crime to associate with defined types of undesirable persons by calling such association vagrancy. Some states declare that every person who associates with "known thieves" is a vagrant,[39] and about half the states seek in their vagrancy laws to

[37] *State v. Harlowe*, 174 Wash. 227, 233, 24 P. 2d 601, 603 (1933). For similar holdings see *Ex parte Strittmatter*, 58 Tex. Crim. 156, 124 S.W. 906 (1910); *Ex parte Karnstrom*, 297 Mo. 384, 249 S.W. 595 (1923); *Ex parte Clancy*, 112 Kan. 247, 210 Pac. 487 (1922). Consult Forrest W. Lacey, "Vagrancy and Other Crimes of Personal Condition," *Harvard Law Review*, LXVI (May, 1953), 1203–26. For a holding that a vagrancy statute is unconstitutional for requiring every adult male to work lawfully 36 hours per week, see *Ex parte Hudgins*, 86 W. Va. 526, 103 S.E. 327 (1920).

[38] Note, "Use of Vagrancy-Type Laws for Arrest and Detention of Suspicious Persons," *Yale Law Journal*, LIX (June, 1950), 1351–64, 1352.

[39] See Ariz. Rev. Stat. § 13–991 (1956); Cal. Pen. Code, § 647 (1949); Hawaii Rev. Laws, c. 314, § 1 (1955); Idaho Code Ann., § 76–61–1 (1953); Mont. Rev. Codes Ann., § 94–35–248 (1947); Nev. Rev. Stat., § 207.030 (1957); Ore. Rev. Stat., § 166.060 (1957); Utah Code Ann., § 76–61–1 (1953).

make an association with a prostitute an illegal act.[40] Similar provisions are found in municipal ordinances. Thus the City of Louisville, Kentucky, provides that "It shall be unlawful for any person or persons, without visible means of support, or who cannot give a satisfactory account of himself, herself, or themselves, to loaf, congregate, or loiter upon, along, in or through the public streets . . . or for such person or persons to habitually consort with bawds, thieves, malefactors, or other disreputable or dangerous characters. . . ."[41] That this is by no means a wholly American phenomenon is reflected in the Vagrancy Act of New Zealand, dating from 1901, which declares that one shall be deemed as an idle and disorderly person "who habitually consorts with reputed thieves or prostitutes or persons who have no visible means of support."[42]

Some state appellate courts have sustained the constitutionality of statutes which define vagrancy, at least in part, in terms of undesirable association. In proving that a man is a vagrant, an Alabama court ruled some years ago, it is competent for the state to present evidence showing that he is "the constant associate of gamblers, prostitutes, and other evil parasites on society. . . ."[43] And it added: "There is no truer saying than that 'birds of a feather flock together,' and, in this class of cases, the

[40] See Ala. Code, tit. 14, §§ 437, 440 (1940); Ariz. Rev. Stat., § 13–991 (1956); Iowa Code, § 746.1 (1958); Miss. Ann. Code, § 2666 (1942); N.C. Gen. Stat. § 14–336 (1953); Ore. Rev. Stat., § 166.060 (1957); R.I. Gen. Laws, § 11–45–1 (1956); Wis. Stat., § 348.351 (1951). Such provisions will also be found in the codes of Alaska, Arkansas, California, Hawaii, Idaho, Louisiana, Minnesota, Montana, Nebraska, Nevada, New Mexico, New York, Oklahoma, Texas, Utah, Washington.

[41] Ordinances of the City of Louisville, Kentucky, § 85–12. See *Sam Thompson* v. *City of Louisville*, 362 U.S. 199 (1960).

[42] § 47 (d) of the Police Offences Act, 1927, New Zealand Stat. 1955, II, 1781. Compare New South Wales Stat., Geo. 5, Act no. 30 (1929): one is a vagrant who ". . . habitually consorts with reputed criminals or known prostitutes or persons who have been convicted of having no visible lawful means of support."

[43] *Brannon* v. *State*, 16 Ala. App. 259, 261, 76 So. 991, 993 (1917). But this court has ruled that there is not sufficient proof of vagrancy where the police have merely testified that within the past year the accused was seen talking to men who had the reputation of being professional gamblers. *Snitzer* v. *State*, 29 Ala. App. 597, 199 So. 745 (1940); *Hallworth* v. *State*, 28 Ala. App. 416, 185 So. 908 (1939).

law recognizes it." The Virginia Supreme Court, in 1937, sustained a conviction under a statute which declared that persons who have no visible means of support and consort with idlers and gamblers shall be deemed vagrants, on the theory that its purpose was not merely to decrease the possibility of persons becoming public charges, but also to destroy breeding places of crime.[44] This court stressed the fact that mere consorting with gamblers was not enough to warrant a finding of guilt, since in addition the defendant had to have no visible income lawfully acquired. Similarly, the highest court of Louisiana has sustained convictions under the state vagrancy law where the accused habitually associated with prostitutes[45] or thieves,[46] taking the view that this was a legitimate and proper exercise of the police power's interest in protecting public morals, health, and good order.

Nevertheless, the weight of judicial opinion in the states is the other way. This is reflected in a series of Missouri decisions on the subject. In 1873, the Supreme Court of Missouri set aside a conviction where the defendant was charged under an ordinance with knowing association with persons having a reputation of being thieves and prostitutes.[47] The court held that intent to commit a crime must be shown in association with others before such association can be punished. "So long as the power and right of locomotion is conceded," the court declared, "and a citizen has the right of selecting his associates, it is difficult to see how the Legislature can interfere, upon the mere ground of correcting the morals of the person concerned." Furthermore, it was noted that "the power to arrest for keeping bad company is a dangerous one, liable to great abuses and partial and unjust discriminations."[48] Accordingly, the ordinance was amended to prohibit knowingly associating with persons of evil reputation "for the purpose and with the design and intent," of conspiring to assist them in crime. Even

[44] *Morgan* v. *Com.*, 168 Va. 731, 191 S.E. 791, 111 A.L.R. 62 (1937).

[45] *State* v. *McCormick*, 142 La. 580, 77 So. 288 (1917).

[46] *City of New Orleans* v. *Postek*, 180 La. 1048, 158 So. 553 (1934). See also, *In re McCue*, 7 Cal. App. 765, 96 P. 110 (1908), for a similar holding.

[47] *St. Louis* v. *Fitz*, 53 Mo. 582 (1873).

[48] *Ibid.*, at 585, 586.

in this form, the ordinance was held invalid in 1895, the court ruling that the right to associate is guaranteed by the state constitution and laws, so long as one conducts himself in "a decent and orderly manner," and does not interfere with the rights of others.[49] The following year the Missouri Supreme Court reviewed the question and again held the St. Louis ordinance to be an unconstitutional invasion of personal liberty.[50] "We deny the power of any legislative body in this country," the court declared, "to choose for our citizens whom their associates shall be." The state, it held, cannot punish an individual merely for improper intentions or purposes; there must be proof of some overt act done.

A number of state courts have ruled that a statute or ordinance goes too far in restraining personal liberty if it penalizes any sort of association with common prostitutes. In effect, the Arkansas court once pointed out, such an ordinance "takes from the prostitute the value of the right to reside in the city by depriving her of the privileges which give that right value."[51] The Texas Court of Criminal Appeals thought that an ordinance which made it unlawful for a man to ride with or walk along the street or be together in public with a prostitute was unreasonable police power legislation.[52] It was noted that there were many situations where men might have something

[49] *St. Louis v. Roche,* 128 Mo. 541, 31 S.W. 915 (1895).

[50] *Ex parte Smith,* 135 Mo. 223, 36 S.W. 628, 33 L.R.A. 606, 58 Am. St. Rep. 576 (1896). In *Lancaster v. Reed,* 207 S.W. 868 (Mo. App. 1919), the Kansas City Court of Appeals held an ordinance forbidding association with persons of ill repute to be an unreasonable infringement upon the right of personal liberty. "We deny the right of the city to declare an act one of public indecency where the person involved is conducting himself in an orderly and decent manner even though he may be found in the company and associating with one of ill repute."

[51] *Coker v. City of Fort Smith,* 162 Ark. 567, 258 S.W. 388 (1924). A dissenting judge thought that the ordinance was needed to protect society. He wrote: "Fallen women are unfortunate, and deserve pity, but when they give themselves over to lives of prostitution they cannot expect, and are not permitted, the same degree of liberty as that enjoyed by other members of society. . . . However much we may pity fallen women, it is shocking to the sensibilities to witness the flagrant and needless association of men with them in public places."

[52] *Ex parte Cannon,* 94 Tex. Crim. 257, 250 S.W. 429 (1923).

81

to do with fallen women with the best possible motives—e.g., religious, charitable, or business in character—and wholly without evil purpose. Such an ordinance, the South Dakota court once pointed out, "would prevent personal effort on the part of male citizens to uplift and ameliorate the condition of fallen women," as in the case of ministers of the gospel, physicians, nurses, and welfare workers.[53] In accordance with this view a New York court once ruled that merely because a man is an ex-convict does not support the inference that he is "vicious and dissolute" within the meaning of a statute forbidding women to associate with such characters.[54] The court pointed out that "ostracism is a punishment unknown to our law, and cannot be assumed to have been intended by the Legislature."

The high-water mark in the effort to discourage certain types of association by law came in the 1930's, when several states adopted public enemy acts at a time of unusual national concern with the crime problem. There were a number of legislative precedents in the background: conspiracy statutes, laws dealing with criminal attempts, and disorderly conduct[55] as well as vagrancy statutes. Only the New Jersey public enemy act reached the United States Supreme Court, in the landmark case of *Lanzetta* v. *New Jersey*.[56] The statute, adopted in 1934, read as follows: "Any person not engaged in any lawful occupation, known to be a member of any gang consisting of two or more persons, who has been convicted at least three times of being a disorderly person, or who has been convicted of any crime in this or any other State, is declared to be a gangster. . . ."[57] Penalties went up to a $1,000 fine or twenty years in jail, or both. The Supreme Court held, by unanimous vote, that this statute violated the Due Process Clause of the Constitution, on the ground that its basic terms were too "vague, indefinite and uncertain." "No one," wrote Mr. Justice Butler, "may be required at peril of life, liberty or

[53] *City of Watertown* v. *Christnacht*, 39 S.D. 290, 164 N.W. 62 (1917). For similar holdings see *Hechinger* v. *Maysville*, 22 Ky. L.R. 486, 57 S.W. 619 (1900); *Cady* v. *Barnesville*, 4 Ohio Dec. Rep. 396 (1878).

[54] *People ex rel. Palter* v. *Warden*, 200 N.Y.S. 542 (Sup. Ct. 1921).

[55] Under Mich. Stat. Ann. § 28.364 (1956), vagrants fall under the class of disorderly persons.

[56] 306 U.S. 451 (1939).   [57] N.J. Laws 1934, c. 155, § 4.

property to speculate as to the meaning of penal statutes. All are entitled to be informed as to what the State commands or forbids." The terms of a penal statute, he said, may not be so vague that men of common intelligence must guess as to its meaning. The uncertainty in this instance turned on the vagueness of several key words and phrases: What is a "gang"? What is meant by being "known to be a member"? What is membership and how is it secured?[58]

The New York public enemy act was adopted in 1931 as an additional section of the disorderly conduct statute, § 722 of the New York Penal Law. The new section (§ 11) declared that one who "is engaged in some illegal occupation or who bears an evil reputation and with an unlawful purpose consorts with thieves and criminals or frequents unlawful resorts," is guilty of disorderly conduct.[59] Since it was almost impossible to prove "unlawful purpose,"[60] the legislature added an amendment in 1935 which provides: "In any prosecution under this section the fact that defendant is engaged in an illegal occupation or bears an evil reputation and is found consorting with persons of like evil reputation, thieves or criminals shall be prima facie evidence that such consorting was for an unlawful purpose."[61] This statute was adopted by the legislature over the strong objections of the New York Law Revision Commission, which argued that "the concept that underlies legislation penalizing not specific acts but a course of conduct or mode of life is feudal. . . . It is at variance with just and humane policy,—a policy which finds expression in the principle that an accused

[58] This case would seem to have set aside a decision made by the New Jersey court which upheld the Gangster Act, *State* v. *Gaynor,* 119 N.J.L. 582, 197 A. 360 (1938). The court treated the act as a conspiracy statute, the only difference being that the Gangster Act did not require an agreement to commit a specific crime, but only to engage generally in criminal activity. The language of the statute was held to be sufficiently precise.

[59] N.Y. Laws 1931, c. 793.

[60] John J. Sullivan, "The Public Enemy Act in New York," *Brooklyn Law Review,* V (October, 1935), 62–69. See also Note, "Disorderly Conduct in New York Penal Law § 722," *Brooklyn Law Review,* XXV (December, 1958), 46–72.

[61] N.Y. Laws 1935, c. 921.

shall be specifically informed of the offense charged."[62] It went on to say that the underlying purpose of the Act was "to relieve the police of the necessity of proving that criminals have committed or are planning to commit specific crimes." On the other hand, it has been argued that "it is not unreasonable to presume that when persons of evil reputation consort with criminals some violation of law may result. When such persons are in constant association with each other, human experience records that such association in the majority of cases is for an unlawful purpose."[63] The New York Court of Appeals, construing the act in 1936, was careful to point out that mere consorting with thieves and criminals is not made a crime, since an evil purpose must also be proved.[64] The state must prove that there was an association of evil-minded persons doing or planning to do something unlawful. "The consorting alone is no crime." Thus, to sustain a prosecution, the state must prove: (1) an intent to provoke a breach of the peace; (2) the defendant's evil reputation; (3) that this bad person consorts with thieves and criminals, present wrongdoers; and (4) that the companionship has an unlawful purpose. Said Chief Judge Crane: "Here then is the crime. If a person of bad reputation, with intent to provoke a breach of the peace, keeps company with criminals, makes them his associates, for an unlawful purpose, he is guilty of disorderly conduct." He went on to concede that it may be difficult to find the evidence needed to prove a case.

The Illinois legislature adopted a public enemy law in 1933,[65] but the following year the state's highest court declared it to be unconstitutional.[66] The statute, an amendment to the Vagabond

[62] Report of the Law Revision Commission of New York, 1935, Legis. Doc. (1935) No. 60, pp. 589–622, 590–91.

[63] Sullivan, *op. cit.*, pp. 66–67.

[64] *People* v. *Pieri*, 269 N.Y. 315, 199 N.E. 495 (1936). In this particular case the court concluded that there was not sufficient evidence to sustain the convictions under the statute. Evidence that two brothers previously convicted of motor law violations and two others previously convicted of felonies and bearing bad reputations had been seen standing on a street corner talking was held to be insufficient to sustain a conviction.

[65] Laws of Illinois, 1933, p. 489.

[66] *People* v. *Belcastro*, 356 Ill. 144, 190 N.E. 301 (1934); *People* v. *Alterie*, 356 Ill. 307, 190 N.E. 305 (1934).

Act, provided that persons reputed to be habitual violators of criminal laws or reputed to act as associates or companions of such persons, or who are reputed to carry concealed weapons, shall be treated as vagabonds. In one case the indictment charged that the defendant was a habitual violator of the laws of the state, an associate of habitual law violators, and a carrier of a concealed weapon.[67] The court ruled that this was arbitrary and unreasonable legislation which deprived the citizen of his liberty without due process of law, and that it clothed administrative officers with arbitrary and discriminatory powers, since it lacked sufficiently specific standards. Chief Judge Orr declared: "No legislative body in this country possesses the power to choose associates for citizens. With mere guilty intention, divorced from an overt act or outward manifestation thereof, the law does not concern itself."

Finally, Michigan adopted a type of public enemy act in 1931.[68] This statute declared that "any person who engages in an illegal occupation or business" shall be deemed a disorderly person, and that "proof of recent reputation for engaging in an illegal occupation or business" shall be prima facie evidence of being so engaged.[69] The Supreme Court of Michigan promptly held this law unconstitutional, though by a four-to-three vote.[70] The court held that "the presumption so declared by the enactment is not a rational deduction or inference from fact to fact, but an arbitrary fiat of the legislature." Furthermore, under the statutory rule of evidence, "no man's liberty is safeguarded; for malice, spite, gossip, unfounded accusation, slander and libel, resulting in reputation, will come into court under the guise of fact. . . ." Finally, the court thought that the act reversed the presumption of innocence, for unless the accused enters upon a defense, the legislatively established presumption authorized a conviction.

[67] *People* v. *Belcastro*, see above, note 66.

[68] Mich. Pub. Acts 1931, No. 328, § 167–68. S.D. Sess. Laws 1931, c. 128, § 1, has been classified by some writers as a public enemy act, but it seems to be simply a vagrancy statute.

[69] See Comment, "Constitutional Validity of Statute Establishing Proof of Reputation as Prima Facie Evidence of Commission of Crime," *Michigan Law Review*, XXX (February, 1932), 600–609.

[70] *People* v. *Licavoli*, 264 Mich. 643, 250 N.W. 520 (1934).

Of course, one may get into other kinds of trouble by keeping "bad" company. Under the Smith Act, for example, conspiring with others to advocate or teach the desirability of overthrowing the government by unlawful means is punishable, but the crime is the ancient offense of conspiracy, and does not rest upon the wickedness of one's associates.[71] Or, to cite another illustration, a schoolteacher may be dismissed for associating with unsavory characters, since the nature of her job requires both good moral character and a good reputation,[72] but the discharge is not a criminal penalty as the term is used in American law. While efforts have been made occasionally in various states to make association with defined classes of "bad" people per se a crime, and while a few state appellate courts have found ways of enforcing them over constitutional objections, the great weight of authority is clearly the other way. This is no more than right and proper, since in a country dedicated to respecting maximum personal liberty it is unseemly to make it a crime merely to associate with "wicked" people. As a matter of fact, even "wicked" people have the same elemental right of human association that all other people enjoy, and ostracism or outlawry is wholly repugnant to our moral and legal traditions. It is time enough for the criminal law to intervene when actual actions of an illegal character have been taken.

[71] *Dennis* v. *United States*, 341 U.S. 494 (1951).

[72] *Horosko* v. *Mt. Pleasant Township School District*, 335 Pa. 369, 6 A. 2d 866 (1939); *Faxon* v. *School Committee of Boston*, 331 Mass. 531, 120 N.E. 2d 772 (1954); *Pickus* v. *Board of Education of Chicago*, 9 Ill. 2d 599, 138 N.E. 2d 532 (1956); *Pockman* v. *Leonard*, 39 Cal. 2d 676, 249 P. 2d 267 (1952); *Thorp* v. *Board of Trustees of Newark*, 6 N.J. 498, 79 A. 2d 462 (1951), *judgment vacated as moot*, 342 U.S. 803 (1951). Cf. *Adler* v. *Board of Education*, 342 U.S. 485 (1952).

CHAPTER VI

THE RIGHTS OF ASSOCIATION IN EUROPEAN DEMOCRACIES

THE RIGHTS OF ASSOCIATION IN GREAT BRITAIN

The rights of association, in the various forms they take, are deeply rooted in ancient law. The general view which prevailed in the medieval period was that an association was legal, even though not sanctioned by a superior authority, if its purpose was the promotion or realization of justice, that is to say, the pursuit of a just and righteous cause.[1] But monopolies, criminal or seditious societies, and societies leading to public scandal were regarded as illicit.

The right of the British subject to associate with others, and to hold public meetings and processions has had a long and complex history in English law. Indeed, in a famous chapter on "The Right of Public Meeting," Dicey argued that the English Constitution can hardly be said to recognize such a thing as any specific right of public meetings.[2] "The right of assembling," he wrote, "is nothing more than a result of the view taken by the courts as to individual liberty of person and individual liberty

[1] W. Ullmann, "The Medieval Theory of Legal and Illegal Organizations," *Law Quarterly Review*, LX (July, 1944), 285-91.

[2] A. V. Dicey, *Introduction to the Law of the Constitution,* 9th edition, ed. E. C. S. Wade (London: Macmillan, 1939), chap. vii. See the remarks of Lord Hewart, C.J., in *Duncan* v. *Jones,* [1936] 1 K.B. 218, 222 (1935): ". . . English law does not recognize any special right of public meeting for political or other purposes."

of speech."[3] But Professor Goodhart has shown that Dicey, and others, fell into error because they failed to distinguish between public meetings and public processions.[4] There is a great deal of difference in English law between a meeting on a highway and a procession on a highway, since there is no right to the former, whereas the latter is prima facie lawful. It has been persuasively argued that the right of assembly is part of both English common and statutory law.[5]

Unlawful Assembly Subject to certain liabilities of the ordinary law, English law does not prohibit the freedom of association and the holding of public meetings.[6] It is common knowledge that there are thousands of voluntary associations in England, which are organized for every conceivable purpose, and that numberless meetings are held each year on public or private property for all sorts of objectives. Nevertheless, since very early days both the common law and acts of Parliament set limits to the right of assembly in the interests of public order through the concepts of unlawful assembly, rout, and riot. An act was passed in 1412 providing against "any riot, assembly, or rout of people, against the law,"[7] and this was soon reinforced by a provision making it the duty of people to aid in suppressing riots, routs, and illegal assemblies.[8] As a consequence of the many tumults and insurrections which were triggered by the enclosure movement, a statute was passed in the reign of Edward VI making it a felony for twelve or more people to meet together for the object of destroying enclosures,

[3] *Ibid.*, p. 271. For a defense of Dicey see W. Ivor Jennings, "The Right of Assembly in England," *New York University Law Quarterly Review,* IX (December, 1931), 217–21. Nevertheless, Jennings thought that Dicey's views, which were expressed in 1885, were no longer relevant to modern constitutional law.

[4] A. L. Goodhart, "Public Meetings and Processions," *Cambridge Law Journal,* VI (1937), 616–74. See also the remarks of the editor of the Ninth Edition of Dicey's treatise on the constitution, *op. cit.,* pp. 553–54.

[5] James M. Jarrett and Vernon A. Mund, "The Right of Assembly," *New York University Law Quarterly Review,* IX (September, 1931), 1–38.

[6] Edward Jenks, *The Book of English Law* (2d ed.; London: John Murray, 1928), p. 180.

[7] 13 Henry 4, c. 7 (1412).

[8] 2 Henry 5, c. 8, § 2 (1414).

and treason to meet together "on any matter of state."[9] Still later statutes were enacted which give Justices of the Peace authority to order an unlawful assembly to disperse,[10] and in the reign of George I the Riot Act was passed to prevent "Tumults and riotous Assembly," as an aid in the execution of the Act of Settlement.[11]

An early common law writer, William Lambard, published a treatise in 1581 on the office of Justice of the Peace in which the following definitions were made:

> An unlawfull Assembly, is the companie of three or moe persons, disorderly comming together, forcibly to commit an unlawful act: as, to beate a man, or to enter upon his possession, or such like. . . .
>
> A Route is a disordered assembly of three or moe persons, moving forwarde to commit by force an unlawfull acte. For it is a Route, whether they put their purpose in ful execution, or no, if so be that they doe goe, ride, or move forward after their first meeting. . . .
>
> A Riot, is thought to bee, where three or moe persons, be disorderly assembled to commit with force any such unlawfull acte, and do accordingly execute the same. . . .
>
> And thus (upon the whole reckoning) an unlawfull assembly is the first degree, or beginning: a Route, the next step, or proceeding: and a Riot the ful effect and consummation, of such a disordered and forbidden action.[12]

Lambard emphasized that unlawful assembly, rout, and riot had two characteristics in common: (1) at least three people must be gathered together, and (2) being together, they "doe breede some apparant disturbance of the Peace, either by signification of Speach, shew of Armour, turbulent Gesture, or actuall and expresse Violence: so that eyther the peaceable sort of men be unquieted and feared by the Fact, or the lighter sort and busie bodies be emboldened by the Example."[13]

---

[9] 3 & 4 Edw. 6, c. 5 (1549).

[10] 1 Mary, c. 12, sess. 2 (1554); 1 Eliz., c. 16 (1558).

[11] 1 Geo. 1, Stat. 2, c. 5 (1714). See *R. v. Child*, 4 Car. & P. 442, 174 Eng. Rep. 774 (N.P. 1831).

[12] *Eirenarcha: or of The Office of the Justices of Peace* (2d ed.; London: Ralph Newbery, 1592), pp. 179–81. Lambard recognized even then that not all men agreed on these distinctions. *Ibid.*, p. 179.

[13] *Ibid.*, p. 181.

Writing in 1635, William Hudson defined unlawful assembly as "when two or more assemble themselves together to do some unlawful thing . . . *in terrorem populi*."[14] But Serjeant Hawkins declared in 1715 that this ancient definition was "much too narrow," since he maintained that an unlawful purpose was not an essential element of the offense.[15] "For any meeting whatsoever," he wrote, "of great numbers of people with such circumstances of terror, as cannot but endanger the publick peace, and raise fears and jealousies among the king's subjects, seems properly to be called an unlawful assembly. . . ."[16] On the other hand, Blackstone defined an unlawful assembly as an assembly of three or more "to do an unlawful act."[17] Though it was once ruled in a well-known case that an assembly cannot be deemed unlawful if it had a lawful object and no purpose to use violence,[18] the view now prevails that an unlawful assembly is an assembly of persons who have the intention of carrying out a common purpose, whether lawful or unlawful, in such a manner as to give firm and courageous persons in the neighborhood ground to apprehend that a breach of the peace will result.[19]

In our times, instead of the common law offense of unlawful assembly, reliance is had mainly on the statutory offense created by the Metropolitan Police Act, 1839,[20] and other local acts, of

[14] *A Treatise on the Court of Star Chamber*, reprinted in Francis Hargrave (ed.), *Collectanea Juridica* (London: E. and R. Brooks, 1792), pp. 82–85.

[15] William Hawkins, *Pleas of the Crown*, 6th edition, ed. Thomas Leach (Dublin: Eliz. Lynch, 1788), I, 297.

[16] *Ibid.*   [17] 4 Bl. Com. * 146.

[18] *Beatty* v. *Gillbanks*, (1882) 9 Q.B.D. 308.

[19] *R.* v. *Cunninghame Graham*, [1888] 16 Cox C.C. 420. See also *R.* v. *Neale*, 9 Car. & P. 431, 173 Eng. Rep. 899 (N.P. 1839); *R.* v. *Vincent*, (1839), 3 St. Tr. (n.s.) 1037; *R.* v. *Billingham*, 2 Car. & P. 234, 172 Eng. Rep. 106 (N.P. 1825); *R.* v. *Birt*, 5 Car. & P. 154, 172 Eng. Rep. 919 (N.P. 1831). For general reviews of the law see E. C. S. Wade and G. Godfrey Phillips, *Constitutional Law* (3d ed.; London: Longmans, Green, 1946), pp. 331–35; A. B. Keith, *The Constitution of England from Queen Victoria to George VI* (London: Macmillan, 1940), II, 408–21; A. B. Keith, *Constitutional Law* (7th ed.; London: Stevens, 1939), pp. 450–56.

[20] 2 & 3 Vict., c. 47, § 54 (13).

using "any threatening, abusive, or insulting Words or Behaviour with Intent to provoke a Breach of the Peace, or whereby a Breach of the Peace may be occasioned." Consider the well-known case of *Wise* v. *Dunning*,[21] which involved a Protestant lecturer who persisted in making public speeches to large crowds in Liverpool, which specialized in insulting the numerous Catholics who resided in the city. The speaker was convicted of violating a local act which prohibited the use of threatening, abusive, and insulting words or behavior in the streets which might lead to a breach of the peace. The reviewing court sustained the conviction on the ground that the natural consequence of the defendant's conduct was disturbance and riot. Under this sort of statute it is unnecessary to prove that an assemblage of at least three persons had a common purpose, since the conduct of a single defendant is punishable. King's Bench went even farther in 1936, in *Duncan* v. *Jones*,[22] where the police had forbidden the holding of a meeting near the entrance to a training center for the unemployed because, on the basis of previous disturbances, they reasonably apprehended that a breach of the peace would occur if the defendant were permitted to speak. Even though no obstruction of the highway or provocation of an actual breach of the peace was alleged, the court ruled that it is the duty of a police officer to prevent breaches of the peace which he reasonably apprehends. Judge Humphreys said that the case had nothing to do with unlawful assembly. It follows that the rule of *Duncan* v. *Jones* shifts the inquiry from the objective fact of what actually happened to the question as to whether the policeman had a reasonable opinion regarding the consequences of the meeting. It is clear that in the present state of English law the police have

[21] [1902] 1 K.B. 167 (1901). See Barrister, "Insulting Words and Behaviour," *New Statesman and Nation*, XII (November 28, 1936), 845–46.

[22] [1936] 1 K.B. 218 (1935). See also *Burton* v. *Power* [1940] N.Z.L.R. 305, where it was held that where a man insists upon holding a meeting, after it was forbidden by the police, at a place and under such circumstances that the police have reasonable apprehension that a breach of the peace will occur if the meeting is held, it is not necessary to prove that an actual breach of the peace occurred. This case involved a pacifist meeting in Wellington, where there was a history of previous disturbances in connection with meetings of the society to which the speaker belonged.

very wide latitude of judgment in deciding whether a public meeting should be permitted, even to the point of imposing previous restraints.

A meeting may be unlawful for any one of a variety of reasons. It may be illegal because the speaker utters seditious words,[23] or because the purpose of the meeting is to promote feelings of hostility and ill will between different classes.[24] Creating a public mischief is a misdemeanor at the common law,[25] as well as incitement to violence. Incitement to mutiny or disaffection on the part of members of the armed forces[26] or on the part of the police[27] is made indictable by statute. At the common law the public utterance of blasphemous words is a misdemeanor.[28]

Public Meetings in the Streets There is no right in England to hold a meeting on the public streets,[29] nor on a common,[30] nor in such places as Hyde Park[31] or Trafalgar Square.[32] "As regards the common law," Lord Dunedin declared in 1913, "I wish most distinctly to state it as my opinion that the primary and overruling object for which streets exist is passage. The streets are public, but they are public for passage, and there is no such thing as a right in the public to hold meetings as such in the streets. . . . Streets are for passage, and passage is paramount to everything else."[33] But Lord Dunedin went on to say: "That does not necessarily mean that anyone is doing an illegal act if he is not at the moment passing along. It is quite clear that

[23] *R.* v. *Burns,* [1886] 16 Cox C.C. 355, 359.

[24] *R.* v. *O'Connell,* [1884] 5 St. Tr. (n.s.) 1, 778.

[25] *R.* v. *Manley,* [1933] 1 K.B. 529, 534 (1932); *R.* v. *Porter,* [1910] 1 K.B. 369 (1909).

[26] Incitement to Disaffection Act, 1934, 24 & 25 Geo. 5, c. 56, §§ 1, 3; Incitement to Mutiny Act, 1798, 37 & 39 Geo. 3, c. 70, § 1.

[27] Police Act, 1919, 9 & 10 Geo. 5, c. 46, § 3.

[28] *R.* v. *Boulter,* [1908] 72 J.P. 188.

[29] *Homer* v. *Cadman,* [1886] 16 Cox C.C. 51.

[30] *De Morgan* v. *Metropolitan Board of Works,* [1880] 5 Q.B.D. 155.

[31] *Bailey* v. *Williamson,* [1873] L.R. 8 Q.B. 118.

[32] *R.* v. *Cunninghame Graham,* [1888] 16 Cox C.C. 420; *Ex parte Lewis,* [1888] 21 Q.B.D. 191.

[33] *M'Ara* v. *Magistrates of Edinburgh,* [1913] S.C. (Ct. Sess.) 1059, 1073.

citizens may meet in the streets and may stop and speak to each other. The whole thing is a question of degree and nothing else, and it is a question of degree which the magistrates are the proper persons to consider in each case, and it is for them to take such measures as are necessary to preserve to the citizens in general that use which is paramount to all other uses of the streets." He conceded that the right of free speech undoubtedly exists, but he noted that this right is altogether separate from the question of where it is to be exercised. "You may say what you like . . . but that does not mean that you may say it anywhere."[34]

It is clearly established that obstructions in the streets are unlawful under the Highway Act, 1835,[35] and the police have practically arbitrary power to disperse a public meeting in a street on the ground of obstruction alone.[36] Furthermore, many local governments have by-laws or ordinances which prohibit street meetings without a license or permit from the police, and these ordinances have generally been upheld against the charge that they are unreasonable and indefinite.[37] The concepts of trespass and nuisance apply to obstructions of the highway. An unlicensed meeting on the highways is a trespass against the urban authorities or whomever is the legal owner, and an injunction lies to prevent the trespass.[38] In addition, it is established that an obstruction on the highway may be treated as a public nuisance.[39] In fact, it is no defense that sufficient passage

[34] *Ibid.* See Note, "Public Order and the Right of Assembly in England and the United States," *Yale Law Journal*, XLVII (January, 1938), 404–32.

[35] 5 & 6 Will. 4, c. 50, § 72.

[36] *Back* v. *Holmes*, 56 L.T.R. (n.s.) 713 (Q.B. 1887); *Homer* v. *Cadman*, 54 L.T.R. (n.s.) 421 (Q.B. 1886).

[37] *Ex parte Lewis*, [1888] 21 Q.B.D. 191; *Kruse* v. *Johnson*, [1898] 2 Q.B. 91; *R. ex rel. Gay* v. *Powell*, 51 L.T.R. (n.s.) 92 (Q.B. 1884); *Slee v. Meadows*, 73 J.P. 246 (K.B. 1911); *Hazeldon* v. *McAra*, [1948] N.Z.L.R. 1087.

[38] *Llandudno Urban District Council* v. *Woods*, [1899] 2 Ch. 705. For other cases involving trespass through the use of the highways improperly see *Harrison* v. *Duke of Rutland*, [1893] 1 Q.B. 142, 158, (1892); *R. v. Pratt*, 4 El. & Bl. 860, 119 Eng. Rep. 319 (K.B. 1855).

[39] *R. v. Carlile*, 6 Car. & P. 636, 172 Eng. Rep. 1397 (N.P. 1834); *Burden* v. *Rigler*, [1911] 1 K.B. 337 (1910); *R. v. Bartholomew*, [1908] 1 K.B. 554, 561.

space is available, since it is not necessary to prove that anyone was actually obstructed. The test seems to be whether the use renders the highway less commodious than before to the public.[40] In actual practice, of course, many meetings are held on the streets in England, and the police are not likely to interfere unless there is danger of a breach of the peace or some serious interference with the normal and paramount uses of the streets.[41] It has been observed by an English judge that "things are done every day, in every part of the kingdom, without let or hindrance, which there is not and cannot be a legal right to do, and not unfrequently are submitted to with a good grace because they are in their nature incapable, by whatever amount of user, of growing into a right."[42] Thus, the fact that a public meeting is held upon a highway does not necessarily make the meeting unlawful.[43] Nevertheless, under these rules the police possess a broad discretion, and the charge has been made that it is often exercised against unpopular political minorities.[44]

Public Processions Processions pose a simpler problem than that of public meetings on the highways because processions are prima facie lawful. Furthermore, unlike the public meeting, a procession is not a public nuisance merely because it creates an appreciable obstruction on the highway. Processions are unlawful, however, if they take the form of a riot or an unlawful assembly, or disturb the peace, or otherwise create a public nuisance. Thus the right of the Salvation Army to parade on the streets was affirmed in 1880's as against the charge of unlawful assembly,[45] and that of breach of the peace.[46] The real problem has been to define what constitutes a public nuisance. In this connection it may be noted that the right of the individual

[40] See Goodhart, *op. cit.*, at p. 165; *Hickman* v. *Maisey*, [1900] 1 Q.B. 752, 757.

[41] See Ivor L. M. Richardson, "The Right of Assembly," *New Zealand Law Journal*, XXXII (Sept. 18, 1956), 265–67; (Oct. 2, 1956), 278–80.

[42] Wills, J., in *Ex parte Lewis*, [1888] 21 Q.B.D. 191, 197.

[43] *Burden* v. *Rigler*, [1911] 1 K.B. 337 (1910).

[44] Barrister, "Police and Their Powers," *New Statesman and Nation*, XII (July 18, 1936), 80–81.

[45] *Beatty* v. *Gillbanks*, [1882] 9 Q.B.D. 308.

[46] *Beaty* v. *Glenister*, [1884] 51 L.T.R. (n.s.) 304.

to use the highways must yield to the public right of user, and that something done by one or a few people may be unreasonable when done by a hundred.[47] Whether a procession is reasonable must therefore be determined mainly in terms of the public interest, and not that of the members of the procession. Thus, in a leading case involving the legality of a procession in terms of obstruction of the highway, the court made it clear that the test of illegality is not mere obstruction, but rather whether the procession constituted a reasonable use of the highway under all the circumstances.[48] The court said: "Occasion, duration of the user, place, and hour must be considered; and we must ask was the obstruction trivial, casual, temporary, and without wrongful intent. The matter is very much one of degree. . . ."[49]

Section 3 (1) of the Public Order Act, 1936,[50] in codifying previous statutes relating to public processions, clarifies the powers of the police where disorder is involved. It states that "if the chief officer of police, having regard to the time or place at which and the circumstances in which any public procession is taking place or is intended to take place and to the route taken or proposed to be taken by the procession, has reasonable ground for apprehending that the procession may occasion serious public disorder, he may give directions imposing upon the persons organizing or taking part in the procession such conditions as appear to him necessary for the preservation of public order, including conditions prescribing the route to be taken by the procession and conditions prohibiting the procession from entering any public place specified in the directions." The immediate occasion for this statute was the serious disorder on the streets of London arising from the clash of different extremist groups, particularly the Communists and Fascists.

A new paragraph, § 3 (2), provides that outside the Metropolitan Police District "if at any time the chief officer of police is of opinion that by reason of particular circumstances existing

[47] *Goodhart, op. cit.,* p. 171.

[48] *Lowdens* v. *Keaveney,* [1903] 2 Ir. R. 82.

[49] *Ibid.,* at p. 90, *per* Gibson, J.

[50] 1 Edw. 8 & 1 Geo. 6, c. 6. It has been held that this statute does not apply to "abusive language between neighbors," *Wilson* v. *Skeock,* [1949] W.N. 203 (K.B.)

in any borough or urban districts" the powers conferred by
§ 3 (1) are not sufficient "to enable him to prevent serious public disorder," he shall apply to his local council for an order
prohibiting, for a period not exceeding three months, the holding of all public processions or any class of public processions.
With the approval of a Secretary of State the council may make
the order. Furthermore, under § 3 (3), which applies only to
the Metropolitan Police District, if the Commissioner of Police
"is of opinion" that his powers under § 3 (1) are inadequate, he
applies directly to the Secretary of State for an order prohibiting all or certain classes of processions for a period not over
three months. It will be observed that under § 3 (2) and (3) the
police chief does not need to have "reasonable ground" for
apprehending disorder; he need only have an "opinion" that a
breach of the peace will occur before he applies for his order.

Public Meetings on Private Premises Unlike street meetings, indoor meetings are prima facie lawful. Formerly disturbance of a public meeting was an offense only if it constituted a
breach of the peace.[51] But in the Public Meeting Act, 1908,[52]
Parliament provided: "Any person who at a lawful public
meeting acts in a disorderly manner for the purpose of prevent-
ing the transaction of the business for which the meeting was
called together shall be guilty of an offence," made punishable
summarily, and any person who incites others to commit this
offence is equally culpable. In addition, more severe penalties
under the Corrupt and Illegal Practices Prevention Act, 1883,[53]
were prescribed for those who commit this offense at a political
meeting in the course of a parliamentary election.[54] The Public
Meeting Act, 1908, however, became a dead letter because it
failed to give the police the power to arrest offenders without
warrant. This was corrected by § 6 of the Public Order Act,
1936, which provides that if any constable "reasonably sus-
pects" any person of committing an offense under the Public
Meeting Act, 1908, he may on the request of the chairman of
the meeting require that person to give his name and address
immediately, and if that person refuses or gives a false name

[51] *Wooding* v. *Oxley*, 9 Car. & P. 1, 173 Eng. Rep. 714 (N.P. 1839).

[52] 8 Edw. 7, c. 66.   [53] 46 & 47 Vict., c. 51.

[54] The wilful disturbance of a lawful religious assemblage was made a
misdemeanor by 52 Geo. 3, c. 155, § 12 (1812).

and address, the constable may arrest without warrant and the offender is then subject to summary punishment.

Furthermore, under the doctrine of *Thomas* v. *Sawkins*,[55] the police may, in the execution of their duty to prevent the commission of any offense or breach of the peace, enter and remain on the premises of a meeting held in a private hall. Said Lord Hewart, C.J.: ". . . It is part of the preventive power, and, therefore, part of the preventive duty, of the police, in cases where there are such reasonable grounds of apprehension as the justices have found here, to enter and remain on private premises. . . . It seems to me that a police officer has ex virtute officii full right so to act when he has reasonable ground for believing that an offence is imminent or is likely to be committed." It is worth noting that under this theory the main business of the police, in seeking to prevent disorder, is not primarily to disperse the meeting, but rather to arrest those who are responsible for the disorder.[56]

Great public emergencies generate their own stern solutions to the problems of public order created by public meetings. During World War I the various Defence of the Realm Acts gave the executive very broad powers to suppress meetings which might lead to grave disorder, breach of the peace, or disaffection, and these powers were used, though very sparingly, mainly in connection with anticonscription and pacifist meetings.[57] After World War I, the Emergency Powers Act, 1920,[58] authorized the regulation of meetings in case of emergency interfering with the "essentials of life." It was first invoked in the course of the great coal strike of 1921, and again in the general strike of 1926. During World War II the Home Secretary was given very broad powers with regard to public meetings, powers which were used against Fascists, Communists, and pacifists.[59]

---

[55] [1935] 2 K.B. 249.

[56] E. C. S. Wade, "Police Powers and Public Meetings," *Cambridge Law Journal*, VI (No. 2, 1937), 175–81.

[57] Dell G. Hitchner, "Freedom of Public Meeting in England since 1914," *American Political Science Review*, XXXVI (June, 1942), 516–25.

[58] 10 & 11 Geo. 5, c. 55.

[59] The British Union of Fascists was in effect dissolved by order of the Home Secretary in July, 1940. For later developments see Werner F.

Private Armies The rights of assembly and association were seriously debated in England in the 1930's, largely because of the disturbances generated by Sir Oswald Mosley's British Union of fascists. The most acute problem arose from the fact that his Blackshirts persistently staged provocative processions through the Jewish quarter of London, particularly in 1935 and 1936. The Public Order Act of 1936 was the result. In addition to forbidding "insulting" words or behavior, and arming the police with special powers over parades under certain conditions—provisions already alluded to—the statute forbade the wearing of political uniforms and the existence of quasi-military organizations.[60] Section 1 (1) provides that "any person who in any public place or at any public meeting wears uniform signifying his association with any political organization or with the promotion of any political object" is guilty of an offense. The chief officer of police may, with the consent of a Secretary of State, permit the wearing of uniforms "on any ceremonial, anniversary, or other special occasion" if he is satisfied that it "will not be likely to involve risk of public disorder."[61]

Section 2 (1) of the 1936 Public Order Act prohibits associations whose members are "organized or trained or equipped for the purpose of enabling them to be employed in usurping the functions of the police or of the armed forces of the Crown; or . . . either for the purpose of enabling them to be employed for the use or display of physical force in promoting any political object, or in such manner as to arouse reasonable apprehension that they are organized and either trained or equipped for that purpose. . . ." The courts were given wide powers to dissolve such associations and to dispose of their property, and common

---

Grunbaum, "Civil Liberties and the Cold War in Great Britain," *Southwestern Social Science Quarterly*, XL (March, 1960), 330–37.

[60] See Joseph Baker, *The Law of Political Uniforms, Public Meetings and Private Armies* (London: H. A. Just and Co., 1937). "The Public Order Act, 1936, . . . has been enacted mainly to prevent the militarisation of politics and to make further provision for the preservation of public order, . . ." p. 5.

[61] The Uniforms Act, 1894, 57 & 58 Vict., c. 45, § 2, makes it illegal for anyone not in the armed forces to wear their uniforms without permission.

law rules of evidence were modified. Furthermore, § 5 of the Act gave the High Court power to grant search warrants if "satisfied . . . that there is reasonable ground for suspecting" that an offense under this section has been committed. Finally, § 4 (1) stipulates that "any person who, while present at any public meeting or on the occasion of any public procession, has with him any offensive weapon, otherwise than in pursuance of lawful authority, shall be guilty of an offence."

In addition, older statutes are still in effect which have some relevance to the problem of the private political army, including the Statute of Northampton, 1328,[62] which prohibits riding or going armed in public; the Unlawful Societies Act, 1799;[63] the Unlawful Oaths Act, 1797,[64] which outlaws every society which requires its members to bind themselves by oath "to engage in any mutinous or seditious purpose; or to disturb the publick peace, . . . or to obey the orders or commands of any . . . body of men not lawfully constituted;" and not to reveal "or give evidence against any . . . person; or . . . any unlawful combination or confederacy"; and the Unlawful Drilling Act, 1819,[65] which outlaws unauthorized assemblies meeting "for the purpose of training" in "the use of arms, or for . . . practising military exercise."[66]

The Right of Association: Trade Unions Mr. A. B. Keith writes in his treatise on English constitutional law: "The right of association is derived from (1) the freedom to contract under common law, (2) the power to form trusts freely, (3) the right to form companies, and (4) the special privileges given to trade unions, taken in conjunction with the laxity of the law of

[62] 2 Edw. 3. For modern prosecutions under this Act see *R. v. Meade*, 19 T.L.R. 540 (N.P. 1903); *King v. Smith*, [1914] 2 Ir. R. 190.

[63] 39 Geo. 3, c. 79. This statute was aimed at "societies established for seditious and treasonable purposes," and to prevent "treasonable and seditious practices." See *Luby v. Warwickshire Miners' Assoc.*, [1912] 2 Ch. 371.

[64] 37 Geo. 3, c. 123. See *R. v. Dixon*, 6 Car. & P. 601, 172 Eng. Rep. 1383 (N.P. 1834); *R. v. Marks*, 3 East 157, 102 Eng. Rep. 557 (K.B. 1802).

[65] 60 Geo. 3 & 1 Geo. 4, c. 1. See *Redford v. Birley*, 3 Stark. 76, 171 Eng. Rep. 773 (N.P. 1822).

[66] *Ibid.*, § 1. For prosecutions under the Act, see *Gogarty v. Queen*, 3 Cox C.C. 306 (Q.B. 1849); *R. v. Hunt*, 3 Cox C.C. 215 (N.P. 1848).

conspiracy."[67] The principal issue in connection with the right of association has been concerned with defining the legal position of trade unions, which were, generally speaking, illegal under the common law.[68] The trade union as we know it today was legalized by a long succession of acts of Parliament beginning with the Trade Union Act, 1871,[69] which freed the unions from the law dealing with restraint of trade, and permitted them, if registered, to vest their property in trustees who were made answerable for embezzlement. The Conspiracy and Protection of Property Act, 1875,[70] provided that it was not a crime to combine to do any act which would not be punishable if done by an individual, and legalized peaceful picketing. Following several court decisions which imposed liability upon trade unions for inducing breach of contract[71] and for inducing third parties not to deal with or work for someone,[72] culminating in the celebrated Taff Vale Case,[73] which held that an unincorporated trade union could be held liable in tort for what its officers did in the course of a strike, Parliament enacted the Trade Disputes Act, 1906,[74] which had the effect of setting these decisions aside. It also set aside several court decisions[75] which had construed the right of peaceful picketing very narrowly. While the Trade Disputes and Trade Unions Act, 1927[76] forbids general strikes designed to coerce the government, it is now clear that in England trade unions are perfectly legal associations in respect to most of their activities. In fact, while subject to some disabilities, for example, as regards compulsory levies for political purposes, the trade union has certain privileges, such as freedom from legal actions brought to enforce

[67] Keith, *op. cit.*, p. 454.

[68] On the illegality of strikes see *R.* v. *Rowlands*, [1851] 5 Cox C.C. 466; *R.* v. *Duffield*, [1851] 5 Cox C.C. 404.

[69] 34 & 35 Vict., c. 31.   [70] 38 & 39 Vict., c. 86.

[71] *Temperton* v. *Russell*, [1893] 1 Q.B. 715.

[72] *Quinn* v. *Leathem*, [1901] A.C. 495.

[73] [1901] A.C. 426.   [74] 6 Edw. 7, c. 47.

[75] *Lyons* v. *Wilkins*, [1899] 1 Ch. 255; *Charnock* v. *Court*, [1899] 2 Ch. 35.

[76] 17 & 18 Geo. 5, c. 22.

any agreement made for the purpose of carrying out any purposes of the union.[77]

FREEDOM OF ASSOCIATION IN WESTERN EUROPE

A guaranty of freedom of association has become a familiar part of the public law of Western European countries, and has its place in a growing body of supra-national documents dealing with civil liberties.[78] Article 20 of the Universal Declaration of Human Rights, adopted by the General Assembly of the United Nations on December 10, 1948, provides:

1. Everyone has the right to freedom of peaceful assembly and association.

2. No one may be compelled to belong to an association.

The draft Covenant on Civil and Political Rights, most of which reached its present form by the end of 1954,[79] spells out in greater detail the rights of peaceful assembly and of association (Articles 20 and 21), but it is clearly recognized that these rights are subject to restrictions imposed by law "which are necessary in a democratic society in the interests of national security or public safety, public order, the protection of public health or morals or the protection of the rights and freedoms of others."[80]

Furthermore, on November 4, 1950, in Rome, the members of the Council of Europe signed a Convention for the Protec-

[77] *Russell* v. *Amalgamated Society*, [1912] A.C. 421; *Baker* v. *Ingall*, [1911] 2 K.B. 132.

[78] See Norman S. Marsh, "Civil Liberties in Europe," *Law Quarterly Review*, LXXV (October, 1959), 530–52; Quincy Wright, "Freedom and Human Rights under International Law," Hubert W. Briggs, "The 'Rights of Aliens' and International Protection of Human Rights," and Mario Einaudi, "Problems of Freedom in Postwar Europe, 1945–1957," in Milton R. Konvitz and Clinton Rossiter (eds.), *Aspects of Liberty* (Ithaca: Cornell University Press, 1958), pp. 181–211, 213–31, 255–83.

[79] See James Frederick Green, *The United Nations and Human Rights* (Washington: The Brookings Institution, 1956), pp. 31–67. For the full text see pp. 179–89.

[80] For efforts taken in Europe before World War II to prevent the abuse of democratic liberties see Karl Loewenstein, "Militant Democracy and Fundamental Rights," *American Political Science Review*, XXXI (June, August, 1937), 417–32, 638–58.

tion of Human Rights and Fundamental Freedoms which includes supra-national enforcement machinery, and which was accepted by fourteen countries by the end of 1959.[81] Article 11 of this convention reads as follows:

1. Everyone has the right to freedom of peaceful assembly and to freedom of association with others, including the right to form and to joint trade unions for the protection of his interests.

2. No restrictions shall be placed on the exercise of these rights other than such as are prescribed by law and are necessary in a democratic society in the interests of national security or public safety, for the prevention of disorder or crime, for the protection of health or morals or for the protection of the rights and freedoms of others. This Article shall not prevent the imposition of lawful restrictions on the exercise of these rights by members of the armed forces, of the police or of the administration of the State.

An interesting example of the invocation of the procedures of this Convention occurred when the Constitutional Court of the Federal Republic of Germany, on August 17, 1956, dissolved the German Communist Party. While the Basic Law of the Republic permits the free formation of political parties, it goes on to declare: "Parties which, according to their aims and the behaviour of their members, seek to impair or abolish the free and democratic basic order or to jeopardize the existence of the Federal Republic of Germany, shall be unconstitutional."[82] The Federal Constitutional Court is given the power to make this decision. On July 20, 1957, the European Commission on Human Rights held that the complaint of the Communist Party of Germany was inadmissible on the basis of the European Convention. In this case the German Constitutional Court did not say that a mere association of people holding certain views was unconstitutional, nor on the other hand that to be

[81] For the text see *American Journal of International Law*, XLV (Supp. 1951), 24–39.

[82] Article 21 (2); for the text see Amos J. Peaslee, *Constitutions of Nations* (2d ed.; The Hague: Martinus Nijhoff, 1956), II, 34. For a discussion of the case of the German Communist Party see: Michael Leifer, "Human Rights in the European Community," *Australian Outlook*, XV (August, 1961), 169–87; see also A. H. Robertson, "The European Court of Human Rights," *American Journal of Comparative Law*, IX (Winter, 1960), 1–28.

illegal an association must commit some overt act leading toward a crime. Nor did it hold that a party is unconstitutional merely because it does not accept the principles of democracy. But it did rule that it must also be shown that the party had an active, aggressive attitude toward the existing order. Attention was drawn by the European Commission on Human Rights to Article 17 of the Convention, which provides that "nothing in this Convention may be interpreted as implying for any State, group or person any right to engage in any activity or perform any act aimed at the destruction of any of the rights and freedoms set forth herein. . . ." In this connection the Commission ruled out the possible distinction between the short term legal aims and the ultimate objectives of the Communist Party.

Western European constitutions now generally contain provisions regarding the right of association. Thus the new Italian Constitution (Article 18), provides that "citizens have the right freely to form associations, without authorization, for ends which are not forbidden to individuals by penal law." But it goes on to say that "secret associations and those which pursue, even indirectly, political ends through organizations of a military character are prohibited."[83] One generation of Fascism was enough. Article 4 of the new French Constitution declares that "political parties and groups shall be instrumental in the expression of the suffrage. They shall be formed freely and shall carry on their activities freely. They must respect the principles of national sovereignty and democracy."[84]

To cite an older democratic constitution, it is of interest to note what the Danish Constitution (Article 78) has to say on this subject:

1. The citizens shall be entitled without previous permission to form associations for any lawful purpose.

2. Associations employing violence, or aiming at attaining their object by violence, by instigation to violence, or by similar punishable influence on people of other views, shall be dissolved by judgment.

3. No association shall be dissolved by any government [i.e., executive] measure. However, an association may be temporarily pro-

[83] For the text, see Peaslee, *op. cit.*, II, 484.

[84] See Nicholas Wahl, *The Fifth Republic* (New York: Random House, 1959), p. 104.

hibited, provided that proceedings [i.e., judicial] be immediately taken against it for its dissolution.

4. Cases relating to the dissolution of political associations may without special permission be brought before the highest court of justice of the Realm.

5. The legal effects of the dissolution shall be determined by Statute.[85]

In addition, Article 79 of the Danish Constitution stipulates that the police are entitled to be present at public meetings, and that open-air meetings may be prohibited "when it is feared that they may constitute a danger to the public peace."

CONCLUSION

The right of association is central to any serious conception of constitutional democracy. In the big states of modern times the individual cannot function politically with any measure of effectiveness unless he is free to associate with others without hindrance. In fact, most people find much of their identity, in either economic, social, political, professional or confessional terms, in some form of group activity. "If we are individualists now," Ernest Barker once observed, "we are corporate individualists. Our 'individuals' are becoming groups."[86] It follows that government has an obligation to protect the right of association from invasion, and to refrain from making inroads into that right through its own activities. While American courts have been dealing with many significant problems relating to the right of association only in the past few years, such cognate rights as those of peaceable assembly and public meeting have deep roots in the American experience, and a well-recognized place in our public law. The modern right of association has therefore developed in a friendly environment.

As the courts devote more and more time to the emerging problems which touch upon the right of association, it is becoming increasingly evident that the basic problem of defining its scope is very much like the problem of spelling out the metes and bounds of any similar right. It is clear now that the right of association, however valuable it may be, is no more

[85] See Peaslee, *op. cit.*, I, 743.

[86] *Political Thought in England, 1848–1914* (Oxford, 1954), p. 158.

absolute in character than are such hallowed rights as freedom of religion or freedom of speech. We do not, and cannot, in the nature of things, live in a world of absolute private rights, partly because private rights themselves jostle each other, and when this happens, choices or accommodations must be made, and partly because public interests often overshadow private interests in specific situations. While some Justices on the Supreme Court persist in arguing the impropriety of balancing private rights against public interests, a majority of the Court is clearly committed to the process of making choices between presumptively valid but competing interests. Just as free speech, for example, ends where libel or sedition begins, so the Court recognizes that the right of association ends where the law of criminal conspiracy begins.

But the right of association matters a great deal, and it therefore follows that the law should regard with great suspicion any attempt to denigrate the right. Doubts should be resolved in its favor, never against it, since the right of association is the rule, and at best restraints upon it are only exceptions, each of which requires specific and convincing justification. Nevertheless, there are vital public interests in the maintenance of law and order, and in restraining criminal conspiracies, and where such interests exist the right of association must yield. The situations in which the problem of drawing lines exists are numerous and complex, and our courts pretty obviously have a job of formidable proportions on their hands.

INDEX

107